SpringerBriefs in Philosophy

SpringerBriefs present concise summaries of cutting-edge research and practical applications across a wide spectrum of fields. Featuring compact volumes of 50 to 125 pages, the series covers a range of content from professional to academic. Typical topics might include:

- A timely report of state-of-the art analytical techniques
- A bridge between new research results, as published in journal articles, and a contextual literature review
- A snapshot of a hot or emerging topic
- An in-depth case study or clinical example
- A presentation of core concepts that students must understand in order to make independent contributions

SpringerBriefs in Philosophy cover a broad range of philosophical fields including: Philosophy of Science, Logic, Non-Western Thinking and Western Philosophy. We also consider biographies, full or partial, of key thinkers and pioneers.

SpringerBriefs are characterized by fast, global electronic dissemination, standard publishing contracts, standardized manuscript preparation and formatting guidelines, and expedited production schedules. Both solicited and unsolicited manuscripts are considered for publication in the SpringerBriefs in Philosophy series. Potential authors are warmly invited to complete and submit the Briefs Author Proposal form. All projects will be submitted to editorial review by external advisors.

SpringerBriefs are characterized by expedited production schedules with the aim for publication 8 to 12 weeks after acceptance and fast, global electronic dissemination through our online platform SpringerLink. The standard concise author contracts guarantee that

- an individual ISBN is assigned to each manuscript
- each manuscript is copyrighted in the name of the author
- the author retains the right to post the pre-publication version on his/her website or that of his/her institution.

Menachem Fisch

Reflexive Emotions

Shame, Humor, Humility

 Springer

Menachem Fisch
The Cohn Institute for History and Philosophy of Science
Tel Aviv University
Tel Aviv, Israel

ISSN 2211-4548   ISSN 2211-4556   (electronic)
SpringerBriefs in Philosophy
ISBN 978-3-031-83766-1   ISBN 978-3-031-83764-7   (eBook)
https://doi.org/10.1007/978-3-031-83764-7

© The Editor(s) (if applicable) and The Author(s), under exclusive license to Springer Nature Switzerland AG 2025

This work is subject to copyright. All rights are solely and exclusively licensed by the Publisher, whether the whole or part of the material is concerned, specifically the rights of translation, reprinting, reuse of illustrations, recitation, broadcasting, reproduction on microfilms or in any other physical way, and transmission or information storage and retrieval, electronic adaptation, computer software, or by similar or dissimilar methodology now known or hereafter developed.
The use of general descriptive names, registered names, trademarks, service marks, etc. in this publication does not imply, even in the absence of a specific statement, that such names are exempt from the relevant protective laws and regulations and therefore free for general use.
The publisher, the authors and the editors are safe to assume that the advice and information in this book are believed to be true and accurate at the date of publication. Neither the publisher nor the authors or the editors give a warranty, expressed or implied, with respect to the material contained herein or for any errors or omissions that may have been made. The publisher remains neutral with regard to jurisdictional claims in published maps and institutional affiliations.

This Springer imprint is published by the registered company Springer Nature Switzerland AG
The registered company address is: Gewerbestrasse 11, 6330 Cham, Switzerland

If disposing of this product, please recycle the paper.

Acknowledgments

This study owes its final version to the keen discussions I enjoyed at a number of forums and gatherings in which I presented early versions of some of its chapters, and to enormously helpful criticism I received from several friends and colleagues. Among the former I would like to mention the conference on "Stolz und Demut. Zur emotionalen Ambivalenz religiöser Positionierungen" organized by Heiko Schulz, Martin Fritz, and Roderich Barth, Marburg, January 2019; the graduate seminar on reflexive emotions I taught at Tel Aviv in 2020; Berkeley University's Center for Middle Eastern Studies, where I presented in March 2021; The World Congress of Jewish Studies session on political philosophy, August 22; the three consecutive annual Theology and Rationality workshops devoted to religious emotions, at The Goethe University's Forschungskolleg Humanwissenschaften, in Bad Homburg, 2022–2024; the TAU psychotherapy program's research colloquium, where I presented in May 2022; and the Yale philosophy department's post-Kantian philosophy seminar, where I presented in October 2023.

Among the latter I would like to first mention Yoav Ariel, whose comments on the shame chapter transformed it, Heiko Schulz, whose remark on second-order emotions at the first of the Bad Homburg conferences, prompted me to add the chapter devoted to them, and Snait Gissis, whose remark in a joint seminar we taught last year, prompted me to write §3.4. Other people from whose comments I greatly benefitted are Shlomo Biderman, Yiftach Fehige, Paul Franks, Yael Gazit, Simon Goldhill, Aviad Kleinberg, Nevo Spiegel, Zvi Tauber, Claudia Welz, Christian Wiese, and Aya Zeidel.

Finally, a special note of gratitude first to Springer Nature's senior philosophy editor Christopher Coughlin, and production editor Thirumangai Thamizhmani and their teams, for their splendid job in bringing this project to fruition, and last but not least to the anonymous reader for press, whose thorough engagement with the text and detailed comments helped improve it considerably.

Competing Interests
The author has no competing interests to declare that are relevant to the content of this manuscript.

Contents

1 Introduction 1
Bibliography 6

2 Nussbaum in Review 7
Bibliography 10

3 Shades of Shame 11
3.1 Introduction 11
3.2 Nussbaumian Primitive Shame 12
3.3 Halbertal's Twofold Alternative 14
3.3.1 Primary Shame 15
3.3.2 Secondary Shame 17
3.3.3 A Note on Williams 23
3.4 Non-reflexive Shame 25
Bibliography 26

4 Appreciating the Comical 29
4.1 Humor's Double Nature 30
4.2 Theories of the Comical 32
4.3 Two Incongruity Theories 35
4.3.1 Henri Bergson 35
4.3.2 Arthur Schopenhauer 36
4.4 Schopenhauer and Beyond 39
Bibliography 41

5 The Humble Self 43
5.1 Introduction: Humility as Emotion 43
5.2 Rationality and Critique 46
5.3 Humility's Dialectic and the Split Self 48
5.4 The Inimitable Value of Otherness 53
Bibliography 59

6	**Second-Order Emotions**	61
	6.1 Emotions *Versus* Volitions	62
	6.2 Judging *Versus* Arguing	64
	6.3 Jaeggi *Versus* Frankfurt	66
	6.4 The Curious Status of Second-Order Emotions	69
	Bibliography	75
7	**All Together Now**	77
	7.1 Introduction	77
	7.2 Shame Again	78
	7.2.1 A Biblical Interlude	80
	7.2.2 A Second Biblical Interlude	81
	7.2.3 The Inner Self	83
	7.2.4 The Joke's on Us	85
	7.3 In My Humble Opinion	89
	7.3.1 Accomplishing the Tricolor	91
	7.4 Buridan's Meta-Ass	93
	7.4.1 A Final Biblical Interlude	95
	7.5 The We in the I	97
	Bibliography	99

Index 101

Chapter 1
Introduction

Abstract This chapter outlines the philosophical project of examining four specific orders of reflexive emotional response: shame, humor, humility, and second-order emotions, which it argues are inherently and universally human, regardless of their diverse cultural and historical forms of expressions. While cultural circumstance and context shape what they respond to, the capacity to feel these emotions, it argues, is fundamental to human nature. It frames the study's philosophical approach by distinguishing it from psychological and linguistic analyses of the emotions under study. The approach to emotion adopted is decidedly cognitivist. It resolutely opposes reductive accounts of emotion as mere bodily responses, in favor of positioning the emotions studied as self-directed judgments rooted in human selfhood and agency. It thus takes a firm side in the broader philosophical debate between cognitivist and noncognitivist accounts of emotion in general. Acknowledging the challenges of evolutionary theory and neurophysiology, emotions like shame, humility and humor, it argues, are critical to understanding the human self and its capacity for rationality and self-critique.

Keywords Reflexive emotions · Philosophy of self · Mind · Normativity · Rationality · Cognitivists versus noncognitivists · Brain science · Daniel Dennett · Space of reasons · Evolution

One way of introducing the philosophical project undertaken in the following pages is to state its basic presuppositions and describe its self-imposed boundaries. It takes the emotional responses it examines—the two forms of shame, amusement at finding something funny, humility, and second-order emotions (i.e. reacting

© The Author(s), under exclusive license to Springer Nature
Switzerland AG 2025
M. Fisch, *Reflexive Emotions*, SpringerBriefs in Philosophy,
https://doi.org/10.1007/978-3-031-83764-7_1

emotionally to an emotional reaction)—to be both inherently and exclusively human. What such emotions react *to* and the ways they are expressed are, of course, profoundly culture- and context-dependent, and, therefore, highly diverse, as is the case with all other emotions. Nonetheless, I take our ability to feel humbled, amused, and to experience shame to be humanly universal, just like our ability to feel, joy or sorrow, regardless of what different cultures at different times regard differently as shameful, amusing, humbling, fearful, joyous and sad. The following pages focus philosophically on the former, while leaving to others the essentially historical task of charting the latter.

The book also leaves to others the complex history of how emotion in general, and those under consideration in particular were conceived in different cultures and at different times. As I shall argue, the emotions discussed here, are not only humanly universal, but go to the heart of our humanity (shame to our selfhood and normativity, humor to our ability to conceptualize, humility to our rationality and ability to self-critique—all exclusively human capacities). How they are *envisioned*, however, depends on how human selfhood, rationality, agency, normativity, and even emotion itself are understood at any time, all of which, of course, also boast rich histories. Here too the present work remains consciously ahistorical—this time, however, with no presumption of universality. My aim is to bring the knowingly latter-day picture of human self and mind to which I aspire and have developed in former work to bear on the four classes of reflexive emotions I take to be both universal and quintessentially human, well-aware that it is a relative newcomer to field.

There is little if any confusion in the literature between the essentially historical and ever-changing nature of what different cultures in different eras deemed to be shameful, amusing and humbling, and that of the nature of the emotional responses themselves. But that is not always the case with regard to distinguishing between those emotional responses and how they were *conceived* in different times; between conceptions of the human self and the human self itself, as it were, which are frequently run together (as we shall see in discussing Bernard Williams's influential *Shame and Necessity*, below Sect. 3.3.3.).

For this reason, neither is the argument that follows made anywhere to rest on how people, today or yesterday, use the terms under study in everyday language. This is not a study in the natural language philosophical tradition. It purports to offer analyses of the emotions it studies based on a philosophical account of normativity, rationality, criticism, agency and self that is argued for against other philosophical accounts, rather than everyday understandings or linguistic usage. (Just as scientific theories of space-time, energy, evolution and social group dynamics are made to prove their mettle in scientific discourse while remaining knowingly indifferent to how these terms are employed in common parlance.) Thus, for example,[1] no attempt is made to look at how the language of shame is actually used. Thus the very common expression "What a shame!" bears no evident relation to the

---

[1] Both examples were suggested to me by an anonymous reader for the press whom I thank for raising the issue.

1 Introduction

conclusions of Chap. 3. On the other hand, the fact that in several languages the word for genitals derives from the word for shame is briefly alluded to in my discussion of shame and nakedness (especially in relation to the biblical story), though not as proof, grounds, or support of my argument.

Finally, despite the book's interest in the self, it is not a book of psychology. It focuses exclusively on the cognitive: on self-reflection, normative commitment, and self-critique and on the motivating force of reasons. It steers wide of the life of the unconscious, and how psychological tensions are met by repression and cognitive dissonance. As I shall explain, despite being spontaneous and involuntary, I belong to the school that deems emotional responses to be a form of judgment (as opposed to mere sensations), and, therefore, as normatively laden, as distinct from desire or impulse—all of which will be further clarified as we go along. This essay does not purport to paint a full picture of human selfhood, but to isolate and study, in petri-dish philosophical fashion, those aspects of the self that render us capable of the type of self-evaluation manifest in the reflexive emotions we'll be looking at.

The philosophical study of emotion has attracted considerable attention in recent decades. The discussion is rich, but, as is the case with emotions research in general, its agenda has to a large extent come to be shaped by a broader and foundational dispute and an equally broad and foundational concern. The two are related despite issuing forth from quite different scientific quarters. The larger dispute pertains to that between so-called cognitivist and noncognitivist[2] accounts of emotion; between those who, like Rom Harré, Anthony Kenny, and Martha Nussbaum,[3] deem emotion to amount to, or at least to irreducibly involve, a form of intentional judgment "directed at cognitively apprehended objects, and sensitive to reasons," Leys (2017, 4) as opposed to those who, like Paul Griffiths and Craig DeLancey,[4] view at least the basic emotions as reductive without remainder to non-cognitive, "subpersonal, hardwired affect program phenomena, each characterized by signature facial expressions and distinct patterns of related behavioral, physiological, and autonomic nervous system processes," as Ruth Leys aptly puts it (6–7).

Within the field of emotion research proper, the dispute might seem to be an in-house affair as to whether emotions such as grief, fear, shame and compassion be conceived and classified among humankind's higher capacities for agency, comprehension and judgment, or as belonging, along with pains and itches, impulses and instincts, to the lower, more bodily forms of human response? However, the more the aggressively reductive picture painted by neurophysiological brain research is endorsed as psychology's ultimate explanatory paradigm, even if only tacitly,[5] the

---

[2] For an authoritative survey and critique see Leys (2017).

[3] See especially: Harré and Parrott (1996) esp. ch. 1, Kenny (2003) and Nussbaum (2001).

[4] See especially: Griffiths (1997) and DeLancey (2004).

[5] Brain science is flourishing with great success, but it has made little if any actual *explanatory* leeway. Locating however precisely which parts of the healthy brain are activated, when we pass judgment, feel, deliberate, decide, search for a word, hold ourselves accountable, assume responsibility or knowingly take action, and when impaired, fail to do so, will at most prove which of them are *utilized* in performing those functions. The difference between knowingly utilizing a

very distinction between higher and lower, cognitive and noncognitive human capacities is worryingly subverted. While most brain scientists prefer modestly not to address the larger questions implied by their approach, some philosophers—Daniel Dennett is a prominent example—treat the implied reduction of all mindedness to the physio-chemical processes of the brain, not as a challenging hypothesis to contend with philosophically,[6] but as the authoritative scientific picture we are compelled to accept without question, regardless of the cost.[7] From such a perspective, emotion may very well contain distinctly cognitive elements, but to no avail, because cognition itself is deemed to be but an illusionary stance, reductive without remainder to the purely physical! Or to use Sellars's well-known terminology, accepting the "scientific image" endorsed by Dennett is to view the "space of reasons" as reductive without remainder to the "space of causes".[8] Hence the pressure on, and the growing tendency to identify emotion scientifically as a noncognitivist phenomenon.[9]

---

device or body part to perform a deliberated task, and a device preprogramed to do so automatically is categorical in this regard.

[6] Prominent among early contenders are Alfred North Whitehead (1929), Wilfrid Sellars (1962), and Charles Taylor (1985, chs.1, 2, 4). Whitehead speaks for all in putting the point thus: "The conduct of human affairs is entirely dominated by our recognition of foresight determining purpose, and purpose issuing in conduct. … As I write this lecture I intend to deliver it in Princeton University. Cut out the notion of final causation and this "intention" is without meaning." To view such intentional action as a motion "governed by the physical laws which lead a stone to roll down a slope and water to boil … is ridiculous. … Yet the trained body of physiologists under the influence of … their methodology, entirely ignore the whole mass of adverse evidence. We have here," he storms, "a colossal example of anti-empirical dogmatism arising from a successful methodology. Evidence which lies outside the method simply does not count." (1929, 9–11)

[7] Because there is a categorical difference between being motivated by reason, acting, even against our will because we deem doing so to be *right*, and being driven by brute impulse or appetite, and because the neuro-chemical ontology of brain processes only recognizes causal motive forces of the latter sort, Dennett and his followers are forced to deny any form of normative self-control or intentionality. We are not selves who use their brains. We *are* our brains! Hence for Dennett intentionality can be no more than a "stance", and our undeniable sense of selfhood and agency, the autonomous freedom of will we possess to pursue goals we deem appropriate, no more than an illusion (or self-delusion) that proved beneficial in the course of our evolution. For a concise précis of his position see Dennett (1987, ch. 2). For a powerful critique of what he terms "cerebrocentrism", see Thomas Fuchs (2021), Part. B.

[8] For Sellars' account of the two incongruous "images" see Sellars (1962). For his notion of the space of reasons see his classic Sellars (1957). For a recent attempt to breach the two spaces, see Furstenberg (2020).

[9] In this regard, Lisa Feldman Barrett (2017) is a promising exception. Though a diehard neuroscientist, her empirical emotions work has refuted the non-cognitivist idea of a bodily or neurophysiological repertoire of fixed and universal emotion signatures, or fingerprints. Emotions, she argues, are constructed (or, as I prefer, constituted) by our individual culture-based conceptual vocabularies. Concepts, in her account, impact and inform the brain processes responsible for emotion, rather than the other way round. Her work purports to set in motion no less than a neo-Kantian "linguistic turn" in brain research, if I be allowed the term. Her theory of concepts (as classifiers pertaining to paradigmatic exemplars), as of yet, however, leaves much to be desired,

1 Introduction

The other scientific concern that impacts the philosophy of emotion is evolution. From a purely brain-scientific, Dennett-type perspective, humankind is in no interesting way *sui generis*. We have larger brains, which, from that perspective, are not qualitatively different from other brains, and therefore pose no special problem for evolutionary theory. However, for those who remain averse to reducing mind to brain and agency to illusion, self-consciousness, normativity and responsiveness to reasons, together with our capacity for conceptual language and abstract hypothetical thought, render us sapiens a kind to itself, and as such a problem from an evolutionary point of view.

The evolutionary problem posed by these singularly human capacities is that of reducing major qualitative developments to the gradual accrual, or confluences of accruals of minute, essentially quantitative, steps. Here, however, unlike the case of brain science, it is a reduction that all involved fully accept, yours truly included. Regarding the philosophy of emotion, the pressure exerted by evolutionary concerns tends to produce contrary responses on either side of the cognitivist/non-cognitivist divide. Because non-cognitivists refuse to class the emotions among humankind's higher and exclusive endowments, their bodily accounts of human emotion render it easily explained as having evolved up from our animal ancestors. But cognitivists have a problem, and as a result, many find themselves having to argue in the opposite direction, mining animal kingdom for rudimentary forms of the kind of judgment they associate with the emotions: the ability to judge an object detrimental to their wellbeing and fear it, to mourn the death or departure of a parent, offspring and even sibling, and rejoice in their return or presence.

Under the long shadow of radical neurophysiological reduction, the broader dispute between cognitivists and Dennett-type reductionists has degenerated into a shouting match. If everything cognitivists consider to be firm evidence of our cognitive abilities—our sense of self, our ability to distinguish true from false and right from wrong, to criticize ourselves and others, to hold ourselves and them accountable, to take and delegate responsibility, and to take theoretically reasoned goal-directed action—can be hailed in the name of science—perhaps the most vivid manifestation of these very abilities!—mere biologically beneficial illusions without remainder, then there seems to be no point to the discussion.[10] In this respect the broader areas of philosophy of mind, normativity, rationality, self, language, and agency have not yet been effected, and with them the philosophical study of emotion. But, at least with regard to the emotions, evolutionary concerns, to which both

---

especially regarding their normative, as opposed to merely representational import. But that would be a topic for another day.

[10] Except for one, which has yet to be fully raised, and is the subject of Maya Roman (2025), namely, that by their very denial of the reality of normative appraisal and human agency, and deeming them illusions in the name of scientific considerations, Dennett and his followers have no choice but to deem the scientific enterprise itself, the scientific image it yields, and its inherently normative process of endorsement, to be equally illusionary and baseless. Or to turn the argument on its head, if the scientific image is considered preferable, because it is *produced and endorsed for good reasons*, there can be no wholesale denial of human normativity and reasoning in the name of science, as Dennett purports to argue.

cognitivists and non-cognitivists are equally committed, have taken their toll. In this respect, Martha Nussbaum's extended work in the philosophy of emotion is a case in point.

Bibliography

Barrett LF (2017) How emotions are made: the secret life of the brain. Houghton Mifflin Harcourt, Boston/New York

DeLancey C (2004) Passionate engines: what emotions reveal about mind and artificial intelligence. Oxford University Press, Oxford

Dennett DC (1987) The intentional stance. MIT Press, Cambridge, MA

Fuchs T (2021) In defense of the human being: foundational questions of an embodied anthropology. Oxford University Press, Oxford

Furstenberg A (2020) From reflex to reflection: moving from the space of causes to the space of reasons and back. Open Philosophy 3:681–693

Griffiths PE (1997) What emotions really are: the problem of psychological categories. University of Chicago Press, Chicago

Harré R, Parrott WG (eds) (1996) The emotions: social, cultural and biological dimensions. Blackwell, Oxford

Kenny A (2003) Action, emotion and will, 2nd edn. Routledge, Abingdon

Leys R (2017) The ascent of affect: genealogy and critique. University of Chicago Press, Chicago

Nussbaum MC (2001) Upheavals of thought: the intelligence of emotions. Cambridge University Press, Cambridge

Roman M (2025) The normative mind. Dissertation, Tel Aviv University

Sellars W (1957) Empiricism and the philosophy of mind. Minn Stud Philos Sci 1(19):253–329

Sellars W (1962) Philosophy and the scientific image of man. In: Colodny RG (ed) Frontiers of science and philosophy. University of Pittsburgh Press, Pittsburgh, pp 35–78

Taylor C (1985) Human agency and language: philosophical papers, vol I. Cambridge University Press, Cambridge

Whitehead AN (1929) The function of reason. Princeton University Press, Princeton

Chapter 2
Nussbaum in Review

Abstract While adopting Martha Nussbaum's cognitivist view of emotion as a form of perspectival judgment, the chapter takes issue with two major aspects of her emotions work. First, while she characterizes such judgments as "eudaimonistic", we deem them to be no less perspectival, yet more generally normative. Second, her almost exclusive focus on the role played by emotion in politics and the law, steers her discussion more toward social norms than to personal commitment, creating a blind spot with respect to the type of self-directed emotional responses focused upon here.

Keywords Martha Nussbaum · Eudaimonism · Animal emotion · Evolution theory · Self-evaluation · Reflexive emotions

Eager to establish a measure of continuity between human and animal emotion—a point made much of in Nussbaum (2001, ch. 2) with respect to fear and grief, and in Nussbaum (2013, ch. 6) with respect to compassion—an interesting blind-spot emerges that pervades all of her extended emotions work. Nussbaum famously defines emotional responses (as opposed to mere sensations such as hunger pangs and nausea), as "eudaimonistic,"[1] as perspectival evaluations, in which, "appraising an *external* object as salient for *our ... well-being*, we acknowledge our ... neediness and incompleteness before parts of the world that we do not fully control".[2] Animal reactions to such external objects, favorable or threatening to their nourishment, survival, or procreation, are indeed *expressive* both of the importance of those

---

[1] Nussbaum (2001, 31–2 and *passim*).

[2] *Op. cit*, p. 19, italics mine.

© The Author(s), under exclusive license to Springer Nature
Switzerland AG 2025
M. Fisch, *Reflexive Emotions*, SpringerBriefs in Philosophy,
https://doi.org/10.1007/978-3-031-83764-7_2

objects to the animal in question, as of its neediness and incompleteness, while humans, as Nussbaum rightly notes, are unique in their ability to articulate and reflect on what they need and what they lack.

But something important goes missing in her account of human emotion due, I believe, to 'evolutionary pressure'. We indeed share with other animals an awareness of, and ability to respond to things in our immediate vicinity that are salient or detrimental to our well-being; things we fear, abhor, adore, need, rejoice in, and grieve when gone. However, in the case of human emotion, characterizing the type of judgment involved as "eudaimonistic" can be misleading. Unlike any other creature, we rage also against injustice, unfairness, stupidity, and rudeness, grieve and rejoice to the annual rhythms of our religious calendars and the faring of our favorite teams, and can be deeply moved by works of art and literature, even when our own happiness, flourishing, prosperity, well-being, or blessedness—the term's accepted semantic field—are not at all at stake. Unlike grieving for the loss of a loved one (the example with which she launches her eudaimonistic account of emotion in Nussbaum (2001)), feeling for the plight of others cannot be easily reconstructed as a concern for one's own flourishing.

Emotion certainly represents a personal perspectival judgment. We respond emotionally to the things that matter to us because they matter to *us*; because we deem them to be important. But what matters and is important to us far transcends the eudaimonistic *per se* to include the entire range of what we care about, and what we care about involves much more than what we need or what we consider good *for* us. We care for what is considered good and appropriate *by* us, even at the cost of our own well-being.[3] Human emotions represent personal, first-person *normative*, rather than merely eudaimonistic, judgments that owe their hold on us, not to the public, legal or social norms by which we *abide*, but to the self-defining norms and standards of propriety to which we are personally *committed*; to *our* norms, to the specific people, objects, events, ideas and ideals we care for and value, to the standards we aspire to live up to, and to which we hold ourselves accountable, not because others hold us to them, but because we deem them to be right.

---

[3] Limiting the objects of human emotive judgment to the eudaimonistic is analogous to the narrowing of those of human reason to maximizing utility in game-theoretical accounts of rational action. Just as human emotion can express a heartfelt judgment related to anything a person deems to be important, thus human reasoned action can be directed to advance any valued objective, profitable or not. Viewing all human feeling as being ultimately about one's own flourishing and well-being, like equating the rational with the profitable, paints human agency as overly and unjustifiably selfish.

Nussbaum, to be fair, makes a point of distancing her use of "the emotions' eudaimonism" (2001, 55) from more bluntly instrumental, egoistic and utilitarian renditions of the term to include "all to which an agent ascribes intrinsic value" (p. 32). But then narrowing it to a measure of the importance attributed to an "object (or what befalls it) among [the agent's] own *goals and projects*" (p. 55, my italics)—an evaluative category different from his standards and normative commitments.

2 Nussbaum in Review

Two of Nussbaum's works' major considerations militate against her adopting such a broader view of human emotion: their focus on politics[4] and the law,[5] and their concern for evolution. To focus on politics and the law is to focus on public, rather than personal norms, on social regulation, rather than personal commitment, on society, rather than self, on group, rather than personal identity. Hence although Nussbaum treats the emotions as wholly personal forms of judgment, when attending to their political, educational and legal significance and bearing, personal emotion is considered mostly as potentially subversive and disruptive of the social and political ideals she seeks to defend and promote. Although she stresses the cognitive and rational aspects of personal emotion, it is their irrational, misguided, even adversarial manifestations that Nussbaum foregrounds. Such is the case with such emotions as fear, shame, and disgust, whose crucially important self-defining and self-preserving roles are all but distortedly ignored. Her study of such emotions is biased toward the psycho-pathological literature, rather than to more balanced philosophical accounts.

Nussbaum's evolutionary concerns, one would think, would serve as a corrective to this tendency. For in animal kingdom all counterparts to human emotion are by virtue of evolution wholly positive. Expressions of fear, rage, grief and adoration serve their bearers well in the service of their well-being and flourishing, and although they are liable to vary among members of the same species, there is understandably little evidence of misplaced, pervert, or otherwise counterproductive cases of animal emotion. Which stands to reason, being little more than instinctive and conditioned by stimulus-response and learning. The clear implication of her work is that whatever sets humans apart from other creatures is responsible for the darker, warped side of human emotion, for which our political, legal and educational institutions must act as correctives.

And thus, overly concerned, on the one hand, with emotional pathologies and their public bearing, and with establishing continuity between human and animal emotion, on the other, what goes consistently missing from Nussbaum's extensive emotions work, is how unlike any other creature, humans are capable of directing their cognizing gaze inwards at, and of responding emotionally to what they feel, know, do, and are capable of. Shame, humility, and amusement, the emotions on which I shall focus in the following pages, all centrally belong, I shall argue, to this reflexive category of *self-referring*, or *reflective* emotions, which when closely studied, can teach us much about what, in principle, sets us apart as human agents from any other animal or artifact. Moreover, not only are these three reflexive emotions exclusively human, but, in their combined elemental focus on self, intimacy, normativity and self-critique, we shall see, they jointly delineate our humanity's very core. Subsequently, these three keen, if wholly familiar forms of self-awareness and spontaneous self-evaluation, together with a fourth class of reflexive emotions I shall explain immediately, can be shown to pose an exceptionally resilient challenge

---

[4] See especially Nussbaum (1996, 2012, 2013, 2016, 2018).

[5] Most centrally Nussbaum (2004).

to adherents of 'the strong program' in brain research—an argument I hope to take up elsewhere.

Needless to say, the exclusively human phenomenon of self-directed emotional response extends far beyond the three specific emotions taken up in the present study. Generally speaking, reflexive emotions fall under two main categories we might describe as first-, and second-order emotions. The former express the pride, joy and satisfaction, or, conversely, the shame, anger, guilt and humility we feel toward who we are and what we do or fail to do. The latter comprise our emotional responses to our own emotional responses. We often rejoice in the joy we feel toward an occurrence, or conversely are angered or saddened by it. We can fear, or despise being afraid, be proud or wary of feeling compassion, be ashamed of a burst of anger or of giggly amusement, and so forth. Second-order emotions, forever reflexive, are no less humanly exclusive than the first-order variety, but they are usually impromptu, momentary reactions to specific reactions. First-order reflexive emotions can be more significant insofar as their objects are more substantial personal or character traits, and their basis long term personal commitment, as when we seethe at our laziness, are proud of our stamina, annoyed by our lack of it, ashamed of repeatedly failing to live up to a self-defining norm, and so forth.

As a rule, first-order reflexive emotions represent a deeper and more rigorous form of normative self-evaluation. Again, they are all exclusively and irreducibly human, if involuntary, and as such deserve special attention. I shall argue however, that the three first-order reflexive emotions discussed in what follows, shame, humor and humility, form a class to themselves in being not only exclusively human, but *definitive* of what constitutes our humanity. Second-order emotions, to which I also devote a chapter, can, I shall argue, especially when negative, display a crucial and equally exclusive aspect of human self-critique. But I am getting ahead of myself.

Bibliography

Nussbaum MC (1996) Patriotism and cosmopolitanism. In: Cohen J (ed) For love of country? Beacon Press, Boston, ch. 1

Nussbaum MC (2001) Upheavals of thought: the intelligence of emotions. Cambridge University Press, Cambridge

Nussbaum MC (2004) Hiding from humanity: shame, disgust, and the law. Princeton University Press, Princeton

Nussbaum MC (2012) The new religious intolerance: overcoming the politics of fear in an anxious age. Harvard University Press, Cambridge, MA

Nussbaum MC (2013) Political emotions: why love matters to justice. Harvard University Press, Cambridge, MA

Nussbaum MC (2016) Anger and forgiveness: resentment, generosity, justice. Oxford University Press, Oxford

Nussbaum MC (2018) The monarchy of fear: a philosopher looks at our political crisis. Simon and Schuster, New York

Chapter 3
Shades of Shame

Abstract Building on Halbertal's distinction between primary and secondary shame (and against Nussbaum's notion of "primitive shame"), the chapter offers a two-tiered analysis of shame comprising two distinct forms of normative self-failing. On the one hand, the shame felt when our privacy is deliberately violated, when our body or innermost thoughts and feelings are unwillingly exposed, and on the other, the very different kind of shame caused by failure to live up to norms we are committed to. The two will be shown to be hierarchically related, and despite their reflexive nature, their different dependence on others will be explored. In addition the chapter addresses the impoverished picture of personhood offered in Bernard Williams's *Shame and Necessity*. It ends with a consideration of a third form of non-reflexive shame.

Keywords Shame *versus* shaming · Primitive shame · Moshe Halbertal · Jean-Paul Sartre · Primary shame · Secondary shame · Harry Frankfurt · Charles Taylor · Self-alienation · Bernard Williams · Non-reflexive shame

3.1 Introduction

Most emotions can be enhanced from without. One can enrage another, cause her grief, endear oneself to others, and amuse and cheer one another up. But in some cases the verb form of an emotion doesn't work that way. Angering a person is to make him angry, but humiliating him is not to make him humble, at least not necessarily. Fury is experienced in response to an infuriating object or state of affairs, the same as fright, dread and joy are responses to frightening, dreadful, and joyous ones. But humility is rarely the emotional response to humiliation. The relation between shame and shaming is similar, if somewhat more ambivalent. Shaming a person may well cause her to experience shame, but most often will not. She will

© The Author(s), under exclusive license to Springer Nature
Switzerland AG 2025
M. Fisch, *Reflexive Emotions*, SpringerBriefs in Philosophy,
https://doi.org/10.1007/978-3-031-83764-7_3

experience shame only if she is shamed for something she is ashamed *of*. This, some might argue, is true of any emotion verb form. A frightening object or state of affairs will only cause fear if we are indeed frightened of, or by it. But then if we're not, it would be wrong to call it frightening. Shaming is different. We are liable to experience shame without being shamed, and vice versa. Shaming someone for something of which she is proud, or to which she is indifferent, will nonetheless be considered an act of shaming despite not causing shame.

3.2 Nussbaumian Primitive Shame

Like jealousy, Nussbaum considers disgust and shame as especially likely to be "normatively distorted," and therefore "unreliable as guides to public practice" due to "features of their specific internal structure" (2004, 13). She admits, however, that "shame is much more complicated" than disgust, because of "its positive role in development and social life, in connection with valuable ideals and aspirations." And yet, she declares, because "all human beings very likely carry a good deal of", what she callsprimitive shame around with them, even after they in some ways transcend it. … shame is likely to be normatively unreliable in public life, despite its potential good. I shall … argue that a liberal society has particular reasons to inhibit shame and to protect its citizens from shaming (15).

Focusing on shame's normatively unreliable manifestations, Nussbaum presents a theory of the emotion's origins, which she locates uncharacteristically in our very biology.[1] According to Nussbaum, primitive shame originates in the jarring transition we undergo at birth: from being "hooked up securely to the sources of nourishment and comfort", experiencing "a true Golden Age" that is rudely disrupted at birth, "bringing the infant into a world of objects, in which it must depend on those external things and persons for its survival" (179). Oscillating helplessly thereon between "fullness and comfort and emptiness and torment", the infant "increasingly aware of itself as a definite center of need and longing," becomes "also increasingly aware of the caretaker as a part of the world that does not always minister to its needs," and develops "rudimentary forms of love and anger toward the agencies on which it depends" (181). Nussbaum's vivid description of how the prolonged period of utter dependence on others typical of human infants gives rise to mixed self-centered feelings of love, gratitude, fear and anger, thus lending the basic emotions a distinct eudaimonistic basis and structure.Shame, she argues, enters the picture as

> A painful emotion grounded in the recognition of our own non-omnipotence and lack of control … [and] a memory or vestigial sense of an original omnipotence and completeness… [that] manifests itself in life. We sense that we ought to be whole, and maybe once were whole – and we know that we are not. … a kind of primitive shame at the very fact of

---

[1] Resting her case, among others, on anti-cognitivist Silvan S. Tomkins' affect program analysis of shame. For Tomkins' views see Kosofsky Sedgwick and Frank (1995), especially ch. 6.

3.2 Nussbaumian Primitive Shame

being human and nonwhole underlies the more specific types of shame that we later feel about handicaps and inadequacies.

This is the pivotal insight on which her entire analysis of shame as a "normative unreliable guide to public practice" is made to rest. According to Nussbaum, all forms of shame have their origin in "primitive shame," which in turn represents a narcissistic inability to accept our inherent human incompleteness and insecurity— to which she adds, referring to Aristophanes' story of the origin of love in Plato's *Symposium*:The way in which [Aristophanes'] speech connects sex and shame seems deeply perceptive: primitive shame is not about sex per se, but about sexual need as one sign of a more general neediness and vulnerability (182–183).

Primitive shame—depicted forcefully by the painting chosen for the cover of her book–Otto Dix's 1926 cruelly vivid portrayal of the distressed "Half Length Nude" trying to cover her naked breasts—is grounded, according to Nussbaum, in a deep-rooted refusal to accept our very humanity; hiding our humanity from humanity, as the title of her book cleverly implies. For Nussbaum one could thus say that in its refusal to accept our very neediness, primitive shame underlies all human emotion.

Needless to say that being ashamed of, and consequently open to being shamed for merely being whom we are, is a poor normative guide to public policy. There is much to be said for Nussbaum's plea to bar such feelings from playing a role in social policy making. People shouldn't be embarrassed by their physical endowments and deficiencies, or ashamed of their cultural and ethnic heritage, nor should they be shamed for them. But insofar as *Hiding from Humanity* purports, not only to deny particular negative and disruptive forms of shame and shaming a formative role in public policy, but to partake in the wider philosophical emotions project inaugurated in Nussbaum (2001), it leaves much to be desired.

In the concluding chapter of his (2007), Moshe Halbertal offers an intriguing analysis of shame, very different from Nussbaum's, as an emotion rooted in "the most fundamental structure of the self" (Halbertal 2007, 142). While Nussbaum sees shame as originating in a primitive, traumatic, and narcissistic refusal to accept our dependency on others, or fall from perfect self-sufficiency, Halbertal sees what he terms "primary shame" as constitutive of, and therefore, as indispensable to human personhood and agency. Nussbaum views shame as expressive of an often self-undermining refusal to accept who one is. Halbertal, by contrast, views primary shame as "as a self-protective emotion in its most basic form" (143) that has nothing to do with self-acceptance.Both view the shameful covering of nakedness as archetypal. For Nussbaum we are ashamed of our nakedness because ourincompleteness is revealed to us by the very form of our bodies with their pointy jutting limbs, their oddly naked front parts, their genitalia that betray our need for one another. ... We sense that we ought to be whole ... round, and we see that we are jagged and pointy and soft and wrinkled.... primitive shame is not about sex per se, but about sexual need as one sign of a more general neediness and vulnerability (Nussbaum 2004, 182–183).

I find Nussbaum's account unconvincing. The shame we feel when our privacy is rudely violated and our nakedness unwillingly exposed is a form of outrage directed at the violator, which has nothing, even remotely to do with our incompleteness and neediness. And the same goes for sex. There are people with whom we are perfectly comfortable in our nakedness and with whom we feel no embarrassment discussing or having sex. Some are embarrassed and others are proud of how they look. At work are social and cultural aesthetic standards, not a shared, inherent bemoaning of human imperfection per se. And the same goes for sex. Some view sex as shameful, but for Augustinian reasons, not because they are, again, even remotely embarrassed by their neediness. In this regard I find Halbertal's account of primary shame far superior.

3.3 Halbertal's Twofold Alternative

Using an image originally proposed by Sartre, Halbertal distinguishes between two basic forms of shame: we experience primary shame when our privacy is violated by others, and what he terms secondary shame when exposed as violating a norm to which we (are supposed to) hold.[2] The image is that of a peeping Tom, who, caught in the act, stumbles in surprise against the door he was crouching at, revealing himself to the naked bather inside. Both feel shame, but of a very different kind. Their different feelings of shame both owe primarily to being unwillingly exposed to the gaze of another—although in the peeping Tom's case, but only in his, the gaze of the other can be internalized, and shame can be felt as a result of self-reckoning.

The bather is ashamed for having been seen naked, despite there being nothing inherently wrong or shameful in bathing privately in the nude. The peeping Tom's shame owes to the disgrace of being exposed as blameworthy. He stands accused by the gaze of those who see him (whether seen by others or himself), the bather does not.

The bather's shame, which Halbertal deems to be primary, owes to being deliberately seen in violation of her privacy; that of the peeping Tom, to being observed knowingly violating a major norm. But in what sense can the bather's emotional response be considered shame? When otherwise wronged, violated or hurt unwittingly, we will normally feel outrage or insult, not shame, unless we blame ourselves for what happened. And yet when we are purposefully observed bathing by strangers, or using the toilet, or even, to borrow Halbertal's examples, singing in the shower or posing in front of the mirror, we also experience shame. Why?

---

[2]Although the portrayal of shame offered by Williams (1993) follows lines similar to Halbertal's, for reasons I shall explain below, he tends to blur the categorical distinction between Halbertal's notions of primary and secondary shame. I prefer, therefore, to set forth from Halbertal's suggestions, and return to Williams's more detailed account further down.

3.3 Halbertal's Twofold Alternative

3.3.1 Primary Shame

Following Sartre's lead,[3] Halbertal views primary shame as a reaction to an assault on our very selfhood. He imagines a nightmarish scenario in which our every thought is displayed for all to see like on a Times Square news ribbon.If a person's thoughts were written on his forehead, exposed before all, the distinction between interior and exterior would vanish, and with it also individuation. Privacy, expressed through the possibility of concealment, thus protects the very ability of a person to define himself as an individual (2009, 142).

All people assert their selfhood by keeping themselves to themselves to some extent, but the vast majority of us do not live completely solitary lives. We engage with others at various levels of intimacy, asserting our selfhood and individuality by controlling to whom we reveal what. The willed play between concealment, revelation and intimacy—determining to whom we speak our minds, to whom we reveal which of our most hidden thoughts and feelings, and which of them do we shield them from, with whom we are physically intimate and to what degree, with whom, in short, we let our guard down—is self-constitutive in two complimentary respects. First, it is the most basic form of self-government, in which we exercise our agency in positioning ourselves in relation to other people according to the levels of access we grant them to the privacy of our thoughts, our feelings, our bodies and our abodes. We do so on the basis of what Nussbaum terms purely eudaimonistic considerations that are not, and certainly need not be generalized or de-personalized by means of anything akin to Kant's categorical imperative; a complex and willed social positioning, by which, in being wholly sovereign, we constitute ourselves as positioned autonomous social individuals.

Conversely, the relationships we forge in this manner, whose thickness is in most cases directly proportional to the intimacy we grant the persons in question, reciprocally define us as parents, children, spouses, siblings, friends, colleagues, fellow religionists, fellow citizens and much more.[4] Moreover, despite being the most basic exercise of personal autonomy and self-constitution, it is only in the presence of, and in relation to others that our very individuality can be established. In Robinson Crusoe situations (before Man Friday arrives on the scene), cut off or banished from human society, concealment, intimacy and revelation are meaningless.

---

[3] Sartre (2018), esp. Part III, ch. 1.

[4] Only in most cases, however. For we also grant such access to certain people with whom we do not have intimate relations by virtue of their specialized capacities. Halbertal mentions undressing for a medical checkup, posing nude for an artist, confiding in a psychiatrist, all of whom we'd never grant such access in other circumstances. (Halbertal 2007, 148). Nussbaum speaks somewhat dismissively of not feeling embarrassed urinating in public in the company of other runners, though she would be in other social settings—but rightly adds, that she would nonetheless not feel shame. (Nussbaum 2004, 205). Halbertal also notes a different category of specialized non-intimate access: those, who are marginalized because deemed inferior, like servants and subordinates, who are allowed to witness everything without causing shame, because they are not seen. (ibid p. 147)

Our selfhood is thus constituted dialectically by being aware of being seen and in control of who sees what. Primary shame is felt when the boundaries we erect are rudely breached. Nussbaum discusses two forms of boundary violation, but misses that of which the peeping Tom is paradigmatic. She speaks of accidental violations, as when a stranger walks in on someone using the toilet, as moments of embarrassment though not of shame. One is shamed, she notes, when deliberately embarrassed:…embarrassment usually comes by surprise and is rarely deliberately inflicted. If we imagine the deliberate infliction of embarrassment, we are moving toward the universe of humiliation. To be seen by strangers while urinating in a public park is usually merely embarrassing; to be forced to urinate in public before strangers is shaming and humiliating because it denies one's choice over the exercise of intimate functions, something that goes to *the essence of humanity*.[5]

The peeping Tom, of course, falls under neither category. He does what he does deliberately, but not at all with a view to embarrass and certainly not to shame or to humiliate the bather he's watching. On the contrary, he observes her hoping to remain unobserved. Nor does he deny her freedom or right to set her boundaries in a way that excludes him, nor does he seek to dismantle them. He desires to breach them, one might say, while leaving them intact. His is the thrill of transgressing an existing boundary, norm or taboo while leaving them in place; feasting his eyes on what he knows very well he is unentitled. Indeed, if such a boundary didn't exist he wouldn't be interested. (There are no peeping Tom's among members of a nudist colony.) This is why his admitted transgression, if exposed, will be the source of his own shame. Nussbaum is right to note that a person who accidently happens on someone naked will at most embarrass, but seldom cause her shame. The peeping Tom does not shame the bather, but still causes her shame—a combination, that by focusing on shaming at the expense of shame proper, Nussbaum fails to register.

Pace Nussbaum, primary shame has nothing to do with social approval or disapproval (2004, 207). It is a wholly reflexive emotion, even if it is necessarily prompted by somebody else. Nor is it due to the false intimacy aspired to by the peeping Tom. As noted above, confined to the arenas of their professional roles, physicians and psychiatrists are granted access to our bodies and innermost thoughts and feelings, wholly devoid of intimacy. In this context, the equivalent to a peeping Tom is an imposter posing as a doctor. The reaction to realizing that we'd been thoroughly exposed and examined by such an offender is not embarrassment, as when a stranger accidentally opens the door to our bathroom, but rather outrage and shame. We are outraged at the violation of our privacy, not dissimilar to when our home is burgled. But the burglar's meditated, rude and uninvited transgression of the boundaries of our private space is different from the peeping Tom or imposter doctor's meditated, rude and uninvited transgression of the boundaries of our very self. Exposure to their gaze is not accompanied by a sense of guilt, as in other forms of shame, but by a sense of defilement. Again, they do not intend to shame or humiliate. They hope not to be detected. They do not seek to eradicate the self. Their forced presence

---

[5] Nussbaum (2004, 205–206) italics added.

within the boundaries constructed to keep them out leaves those boundaries constitutive of the self intact, but undermines our capacity to properly maintain and protect them. It is a more basic and devastating sense of self-failing than the secondary shame of failing to live up to a norm or standard of propriety to which we hold or are held.

Caught in the sullying gaze of the sly intruder, two powerful, highly self-centered, and eudaimonistic emotional responses painfully intertwine: anger and primary shame. The anger directed at the rude and calculated transgressor is inherently eudaimonistic, and not generalizable, as only the fury of a victim can be. The emotional response traces the reverse trajectory of recognition: sparked by the perpetrator's gaze, yet leveled reciprocally back at him. As in Nussbaum's account, it is an emotional judgment directed at an external object. Primary shame, though, is not. Primary shame is self-directed; the reflexive emotion *par excellence*. A self-judgment not of a normative failing or of a physical or mental inadequacy, but of the failing, or, rather, the inability to prevent the contamination of the self itself; a devastating failing of one's very self-constitutive boundary control. No wonder that primary shame can only be felt in moments of rape-like disrespect for the self-making boundaries that the perpetrator must acknowledge and accept in order to disrespect! Shaming and humiliation have nothing to do with it, nor does mere embarrassment.

Nor has primary shame anything to do with Nussbaum's Winnicottian notion of primitive shame.[6] Primary shame, as I have described it, turns on a sense of insult and self-failing, not on a realization of neediness or incompleteness. It has nothing to do with narcissistic delusions of self-sufficiency or perfection. It is to be shamed to the very core by exposure to the uninvited and unwanted gaze of a self-crasher, if I be permitted the term, whose intention is decidedly *not* to shame or to humiliate, only to infiltrate the self's very boundaries, knowingly uninvited and hopefully unobserved.

3.3.2 Secondary Shame

Secondary shame is both different and more straightforward, and in its pathological manifestations steers close to Nussbaum's account. But again, we need to separate shame from shaming, and in this case, as we shall see, also go a significant step beyond Halbertal, and also beyond Williams. In its most basic form, secondary shame is wholly reflexive, and non-dependent on external observers, as in the case of a secret offender caught in the act, like Halbertal's peeping Tom. For reasons to do with the broader questions discussed in his book, Halbertal takes such cases as

---

[6] For her extensive discussion of the case study detailed in Winnicott (1986), see Nussbaum (2004, 189–196).

paradigmatic.[7] He focuses on the role played by being seen by others in both forms of shame, noting, as mentioned above, that in the case of secondary shame, the gaze from without can be internalized. However, secondary shame in its most rudimentary form arises not by internalizing an external perspective, but is wholly reflexive.

Like primary shame, secondary shame also owes to the uniqueness of human personhood, and likewise, to the best of my knowledge, has no parallel in other animals. Self-consciousness, as Harry Frankfurt notes, consists in more than mere awareness of our thoughts, feelings, desires and impulses. It consist, rather, in a form of self-alienation, in which "a sort of division within our minds" is introduced that "establishes an inward directed monitoring oversight."[8] The part that is assigned the monitoring is charged with *normative* responsibilities. It appraises and evaluates one's physical make up, personality and character, desires, impulses, and behavior, judging some desirable and others adverse, some appropriate, others offensive, some worthy of cultivating and promoting, others better suppressed, replaced, or opposed.

To return for a moment to one of the valuable, if underdeveloped insights of Nussbaum's account of primitive shame, for it is important to distinguish between two categories of shame that owe to different categories of self-evaluation. We judge ourselves by the standards we hold to, and often torment ourselves for falling short of them. However not all self-judging amounts to self-critique—a statement that might sound strange to some. Let me explain. We constantly test artifacts, systems, strategies, institutions and people, including ourselves, by holding them up to the standards they are expected, or desired to meet. But to test, no matter how negative the results turn out to be, is not yet to criticize.[9] A pilot ticking through her pre-flight checklist is testing her aircraft thoroughly, just as a reliable dentist performing an annual check-up is running a test on her patients' teeth. But to describe them as criticizing what they're testing would seem quite out of place. Even when we are made responsible for attending to the problems exposed, as when our physician urges us to change our diet in view of our bloodwork, or our accountant, to cut expenses in view of our deficit, they still won't be considered as criticizing us, unless, in addition to urging us to solve the problem, they blame us for it arising in the first place. Criticism amounts to more than a negative test result, it also contains a measure of rebuke or accusation. Objects can be tested, but only subjects, human agents, can be criticized, because only human agents can be held accountable for shortcomings within their domains of responsibility. Criticism purports not only to

---

[7] As we shall see in a moment, Williams, for reasons to do with the questions raised in his book, insists further that what we are here calling secondary shame is never purely reflexive, but *requires* exposure to an even imagined internalized other. The feeling behind every decision or thought that is governed by shame," he writes, "is literally and immediately *the fear of being seen*" Williams (1993, 81 italics added).

[8] Frankfurt (2006, 4). For Rahel Jaeggi's criticism of Frankfurt's account see below Chap. 6 Sect. 6.3.

[9] For a fuller treatment of the difference between testing and criticizing see Fisch and Benbaji (2011, 220–223).

3.3 Halbertal's Twofold Alternative

prove the existence of a problem, but to call its addressees *to task* for allowing it to develop or to persist.[10]

And the same applies to self-criticism. We test and measure ourselves against a variety of standards. Some represent ideals, others, what we deem to be the norm. Some we satisfyingly succeed in meeting. Of some, we fall short—at times, miserably so. It is the latter category of disturbing self-failing that breeds two different forms of shame.

The first, which harks back to Nussbaum's idea of primitive shame, distinguishes itself from the second, that pertains to Halbertal's idea of secondary shame, in lacking any element of self-*reproach*. It is experienced when we painfully fail to meet an ideal or standard we are *incapable in principle* of meeting, and believe we are looked down upon because of it. It is about wanting to be different from whom we are, and refusing to accept whom we cannot *but* be or do. But because we cannot do anything about it, unhappy as we might be, we do not *blame* ourselves for whom we are. We might well feel shame, but, as I shall argue in a moment, it is not fully reflexive. We are not ashamed of having allowed, or failed to prevent ourselves from being who we are. Agency has nothing to do with it, and, therefore, displeased with ourselves as we might be we do not hold ourselves responsible or accountable for it.

The shame we feel, therefore, is not due to a sense of having failed to *live up* to our standards, but of falling short of them as a matter of inevitable fact. (As we shall see in Chap. 5, shame in this regard steers close to humility.) The shame we feel is sublimated. Insofar as we feel it in solitude, it is because we imagine being seen by deriding others; not because we cannot meet our own gaze, but because we cannot meet theirs[11]—which brings me to the main point, and to the key to Nussbaum's lopsided view of shame.

We do not feel this sort of shame when exposed, or imagine being exposed to the *non*-deriding gaze of those who do not hold what we dislike about ourselves against us, and do not consider it an impediment to be ashamed of. In their company we feel at ease. In other words, With regard to this form of shame—on which Nussbaum focuses almost entirely—shaming indeed takes precedence over shame. The shame we feel is internalized shaming. We are *a*shamed, in the literal sense of the term, for being black, Jewish, or gay, not because we accuse ourselves for having done anything wrong, but because we take to heart the real or imagined demeaning gaze of those who hold being black, Jewish, or gay against us. The shame we feel in these cases is reflexive, of course, and is grounded in grim self-assessment (or self-testing, if you wish), but, for lack of an element of self-blame, not in self-*criticism*.[12]

The second form of shame is bred by self-failings for which we not only grieve, but *blame* ourselves. Here, in the inner realm of self-admonition for failing to *do* or

---

[10] A point sorely missing from Popper and his followers' overly analytical account of critical rationalism, that systematically fails to treat criticism as an addressed, norm-laden speech act.

[11] This form of non-accountable shame captures the coupling between shame and necessity at the heart of Williams (1993). For more on Williams's see the following sub-section.

[12] For a different view on the difference between being ashamed and feeling shame, see Taylor G. (1985b, 53–54).

refrain from doing what needed to be done or to be resisted, agency reigns supreme. In Frankfurt's account of the split human self, to assume agency is to undertake to resist the mere force of inner impulse and external constraint, and to be motivated only by incentives one freely deems to be fitting. What renders humankind unique, to use his well-known terminology, is our ability to form second-order volitions. Like other creatures we are driven by first-order desires and impulses, but unlike any other we are also motivated by desires about desires. We promote those of our desires of which we approve and want, attempt to form those we do not possess but desire to have nonetheless, and oppose, attempt to suppress and alienate ourselves from those we deem undesirable.[13] We do not always succeed. Even the most sincere normative aspirations are often defeated by the superior force both of urges too strong to control and enticements too strong to resist. But agency is a function not so much of normative triumph as of normative self-critique. It is by taking a normative stand against ourselves that we establish our agency and normativity.

Desires are not emotions. They register personal pulls and pushes that can motivate action, but in and of themselves, unlike emotions, lack normative content. They manifest attraction and repulsion but unlike emotions do not appraise or judge. Second-order volitions are reflexive. They signal what we want, and do not want to want; whom we would rather be or not be, and as such, by virtue of their reflexivity and despite lacking normative content, they constitute the seat of our normative commitments. The perpetual struggle to impose our second-order volitions on the insistent push and pull of our first-order volitions, gives rise to several reflexive, self-directed emotions: pride, satisfaction, and joy when successful, disappointment, frustration, impatience, despair and anger when not, and, of course, secondary shame of the full self-critical variety. In many cases, there is no need to be exposed to anyone else's disapproving gaze to experience shame when admonishing ourselves for failing to live up to the standards we set ourselves. We do not experience every such failure as shameful. Aiming too high can result in paralyzing self-despair and depression. Getting to know ourselves includes taking the measure of our strengths and weaknesses and treating our normative aspirations realistically. There are things we cannot change, and things that we can. Secondary shame is a valuable, and exclusively human form of self-corrective self-rebuke. It is, therefore, wholly out-of-place with regard the former kind of inevitable failings, even when they are real and disturbing, even when we find ourselves ashamed of them.

Yet, again, we need to tread carefully. Charles Taylor's somewhat misplaced critique of Frankfurt[14] is helpful in this regard. Taylor distinguishes between strong and weak self-evaluations. His insightful example of two diners fighting obesity,

---

[13] Frankfurt first introduced the idea of second-order volitions in his (1971). Taylor C. (1985a, ch. 1) adopts and develops the concept with special reference to normativity. For more on Frankfurt's model of the self, see below Chap. 5 Sect. 5.3.

[14] Taylor C. (1985a, §1.). I say "misplaced", because I doubt Frankfurt would count most Taylorian weak evaluations as more than first-order resolutions of contrasting first-order pulls, that have little to do with second-order volitions. To take one of Taylor's examples (1985a, 31): deciding between vacation options (which, had time and budget allowed, we'd be happy to enjoy all), for instance,

3.3 Halbertal's Twofold Alternative

wrestling with their urge for a second helping of desert, is instructive.[15] The first hates how he looks and is fighting the temptation because he desires to lose weight. The second works hard to keep her appetite in check because she detests her gluttonous greediness. Taylor now invites us to imagine a new drug that regulates metabolism, allowing one to eat to one's heart's content without gaining weight. This solves the problem for the first diner, who'll have no problem filling his plate repeatedly while staying slim. For the second, however, the problem is actually exacerbated. The first diner is worried about how he looks, how he is perceived as overweight by others; but has internalized their gaze sufficiently to feel shame even when he dines alone. The case of the second diner is significantly different. She is not afraid of being *perceived* as, or of *appearing* to be gluttonous, but of *being* gluttonous, or *giving in* to gluttony. The desire to be slimmer, more socially acceptable, to have lower cholesterol, to be rich or more careful with one's money, are first-order preferences we deem pleasing, worthwhile, and agreeable, and the failure to fulfil them, to be frustrating, irritating, discouraging, exasperating, inconvenient, and so forth. The same can be said of many unrealizable fantasies such as being taller, younger, of different skin color, or heterosexual. And Nussbaum rightly emphasizes the grave social consequences of shaming people for what they cannot be held accountable, and the potentially disruptive psychological effect such shaming can have when internalized by its victim.

By contrast, our commitment to acting moderately, to being generous and to bravely stand up for our principles, represent second-order volitions that attribute to moderation, generosity and valor a deeper, self-defining meaning for us than any of the first-order desires or unfounded fantasies mentioned above. And as such, our failing them is experienced not merely as wrong or disappointing, but as a form of self-betrayal, of a giving up on ourselves, of letting ourselves down. It is the difference between merely falling short of our standards, and failing to live up to them. The standards to which we are committed actively to live up define the person we not merely desire to be, but actively *aspire* to be, even when unsuccessful. They represent, not merely the normative yardstick against which we measure ourselves, but that to which we hold ourselves *accountable*.

Secondary shame is experienced when caught in the accusing gaze of witnesses to such normative self-failings, which, in its purist, archetypal form, is a wholly reflexive emotion felt in response to the *self*-critical gaze of our own normative selves.[16] But it comes in different shades. We are not always as perfectly conscientious in our inner dialogues, as when conversing with others. The hold on us of some norms is not always as strong as others, and often not strong enough to motivate us toward what we deem to be good and hold us back from what we consider bad. One

---

does not involve appeal to second-order judgments of propriety, but merely to the relative strength of their attraction.

[15] Taylor, ibid., p. 22–23.

[16] In former work I have referred to the self-scrutinizing seat of our second-order volitions as our I-part: the part of us that speaks for us in the first person, attempting to impose our norms and standards on our empirical selves. See for example Fisch and Benbaji (2011, 254–271).

is then liable to slip into routines or cycles of unchecked normative surrender. The shock of being accusingly seen by others, as in Halbertal's case of the peeping Tom, may at times "trigger a shift," as he has it,[17] in the peeper's self-perception that allows him to perceive himself as accusingly self-watching, as it were. It is in this way that the external observer's gaze is internalized to give rise to the self-admonishing self-critique of secondary shame.

But in some cases, when the blunting of the relevant norms is so far gone and the shameful behavior so routinized, there remains nothing left to trigger or to internalize. Here, the only shame experienced by the corrupt, serial perpetrator[18] is about being shamefully exposed—an emotion unaccompanied by self-rebuke, normative self-reckoning or self-correcting (other than kicking himself for being caught out, and firmly resolving to lay low for a while, and act more cautiously in the future). The person shamed is not rendered *ashamed* of what he's done. He feels no guilt or remorse (again, except for having been careless) only ashamed for being seen by others for the person he really is. In a deep sense, therefore, secondary shame at its lowest, most corrupt and less reflexive manifestation, morphs into a somewhat distorted version of primary shame! For when the offender's normative commitments no longer perform their censuring role, the external observer's gaze is perceived as "violating" the offenders privacy, and is thus rendered, as in primary shame, constitutive of the secondary shame the offender feels.

Primary and secondary shame represent more than merely different forms of an exclusively human, self-directed emotion. Primary shame is indeed primary in being a precondition for experiencing secondary shame. The exclusively human need and ability to chart, maintain, and govern the boundaries of our privacy; to determine and control who'll be privy to our thoughts, feelings, body and home, and to what extent, goes to the heart of autonomous human selfhood. The combined capacity to will to establish such barriers and be capable of maintaining them, wholly absent in other animals, is constitutive of human personhood; a primordial act of agency that establishes us as human agents.

It is in this sense that the primacy of primary shame—the shame felt when the boundaries of our private domain are deliberately violated—asserts itself relative to secondary shame. The capacity to feel secondary shame necessitates an ability for honest self-reckoning that only human agents possess.

---

[17] Halbertal (2007, 143–144).

[18] Frankfurt's distinction between willing and the unwilling addicts captures this distinction nicely. See for instance Frankfurt (1988, 16–19).

3.3.3 A Note on Williams

Bernard Williams's *Shame and Necessity* is a philosophically informed study of early Greek literature, especially tragedy, with a view to countering overly progressivist approaches to the "ethical[19] ideas of the Greeks: "in particular ideas of responsible action, justice, and the motivations that lead people to do things that are admired and respected" (Williams (1993, 4). Williams energetically opposes the progressivist conceit that the Greeks had only primitive ideas of action, responsibility, ethics and justice "which in the course of history have been replaced by a more complex and refined set of conceptions that define [our] more mature form of ethical experience" (5). On the contrary, his contention is that when we "come to understand the ethical concepts of the Greeks, we shall recognize them in ourselves." (10). In a long series of insightful readings Williams convincingly teases out the ideas of agency, responsibility, normativity, shame and guilt embedded in Greek literature, rendering his book a minor classic.However, something gets lost along the way. The impressive enrichment of the Greek picture of personhood he paints comes at the price of depleting the picture we have come to "recognize in ourselves". His account of shame, I noted, steers close to Halbertal's, but it does so with two major differences highly significant for the present study. He too views shame of nakedness as a primary form of shame. "The basic experience connected with shame," he writes,

> is that of being seen, inappropriately, by the wrong people, in the wrong condition. It is straightforwardly connected with nakedness, particularly in sexual connections. ...The reaction is to cover oneself or to hide, and people naturally take steps to avoid situations that call for it" (78)

Yet, despite quoting Gabriele Taylor's pointed characterization of shame as "the emotion of self-protection"—that so nicely captures the essence of the Halbertalian notion of primary shame further developed here—Williams treats the shame of being inappropriately seen naked as that of being "exposed to a desiring eye" on a par with the embarrassment of being (or imagining being) seen making a fool of oneself when stumbling over one's shoelace and trying to recover falling packages (221). Nowhere is the "basic" shame experience of being inappropriately seen naked described by Williams as compromising agency, as a violation of self-protection. It is paradigmatic in involving "a loss of power ...constituted by being seen", not an affront to the very foundations of selfhood.

Second, despite reference to Sartre's peeping Tom image (82), Halbertal's notion of secondary shame is also characterized by Williams as necessarily involving exposure to the real or internalized gaze of another. It is a mistake, he writes, "to suppose that ...the other in ethical [=normative] thought must be an identifiable individual or a representative of the neighbours, or else be nothing at all except an *echo*

---

[19] In Williams's terminology "ethical" denotes "normative" more generally.

chamber of my solitary moral voice."[20] The internalized other necessary for experiencing non-basic shame has to be somebody rather than nobody, and that somebody must be other than me" (84). While Halbertal maintains that the external gaze responsible for the peeping Tom's secondary shame *can be* internalized, Williams views the two forms of shame on a par as *necessarily* involving being seen by real (even if imagined) others.

From the sentence cited above one is liable to conclude that Williams undertakes to paint an independent picture of Greek selfhood, which he will then compare to our own to make his anti-progressivist case. His intriguing discussion of Greek understandings of slavery and subordination of women follows those lines (Williams 1993, ch. 5), because there is a contrast to be made between their understandings and ours. But his discussion of shame moves in the opposite direction. Shame is consistently analyzed and characterized from our own perspective—with reference to our own everyday experiences, ranging from Sartre's peeping Tom, to pettily overreacting to a trivial slight (93), a nude model exposed to the painter's "desiring eye", and feeling a fool for knocking off one's own hat—which is then shown to inform Greek literature in all its richness. Yet while the case he makes for the Greek texts appears convincing, the case he makes for ours does not.

Declaring his intention to counter progressivists by closely examining Greek accounts of "the motivations that lead people to do things that are admired and respected" constitutes the first giveaway phrase. By focusing apriori not on the motivations that lead people to do things that *they* admire and respect, but on those that are admired and respected, willy-nilly attributes (at least) to the Greeks, even if tacitly, an externalist, heterogeneous view of normativity. Williams isn't searching for how the Greek literature envisages the sources of normativity. He has decided in advance where they are to be found. And the allusion to Korsgaard, as we shall see in a moment, is deliberate.

The second giveaway phrase is of course William's above-cited dismissal of the idea that the internal source of normative self-critique can be "nothing at all except an echo chamber of my solitary moral voice," which in one dismissive gesture rids himself of the need to explain why he has turned his back on the entire latter-day neo-Kantian picture of the hierarchically split self developed by Frankfurt, Charles Taylor, Christine Korsgaard and many others, on which the present study builds. The Greek ideas of shame, in which Williams claims we recognize our own, are essentially *not* expressions of normative *self*-failing, or *self*-betrayal at all. Primary shame amounts for him to little more than the embarrassment of indecent exposure, and secondary shame to failing to live up to somebody else's standards—which may very well be a viable portrayal of the Greek view, but leaves much to be desired after the birth of the reflective, self-interpreting, self-judging, and self-governing subject.

From the latter-day perspective built on here, there is no greater normative incentive than one's own normative commitments, which may very well have their origin in social norms represented in and by the various people and cultural settings

---

[20] Williams (1993, 84) italics added.

constitutive of one's maturation and *bildung*. But they owe their normative hold on one, not to their external origin, but to the depth of one's commitment to them. The keyword is commitment, rather than mere compliance. This is the component sorely missing from Williams's account.

So one of two, either Williams, truly opposes the modern view that there is no greater normative incentive than one's own identity-forming normative commitments, which he certainly seems to do, or that he is more of a progressivist than he makes out to be...

3.4 Non-reflexive Shame

By now (pace Williams) the very notion of non-reflexive shame might appear self-contradictory. But it is not. There exists a third, considerably less reflexive form of shame of which neither Halbertal, Williams, nor Nussbaum make mention. It is a form of being shamed, but of a category very different from the type of shaming studied by Nussbaum.

Primary and secondary shame are reflexive emotional responses to what we perceive as self-failings. But we often feel shame for others; not for our own failings but for theirs. As when ashamed of our country's actions or policies, of a close friend or family member's misconduct, or of how our university or religious community choses to deal with a crisis. We are shamed by them, but also feel shame *for* them. The type of shaming contended with by Nussbaum is different. There others seek to make us experience (secondary) shame by publicly blaming or taunting us for what they deem to be shameful conduct or a shameful shortcoming of ours. Here, by contrast, we are shamed by what *we* deem to be the shameful conduct or shortcomings of *others*. There we are shamed deliberately, here, inadvertently. As noted at the outset, shaming of the former type may or may not result in our feeling shame. In the latter case, their shameful shortcomings shame us literally; causing us to feel shame.

But what exactly are we ashamed *of* in such cases? It is not a self-failing of either sort we have dealt with so far. These are not cases of us falling short of normative commitments we hold to or of contending with violations of the self-defining boundaries of our privacy. What we are ashamed of is a subtle and shifting combination of two main elements. On the one hand, we are ashamed of being associated with the individuals, groups and institutions whose conduct we find shameful; ashamed of being related to such people, belonging to such a community, holding a position in such an organization, or of being a citizen of such a state. When this sense of shame dominates, it may take on a measure of self-rebuke and self-blame, not for what they do or fail to do so much as for our connection to them, which is liable in some cases to prompt taking corrective dissociative action. As when we break up with a disgraceful friend, sever relations with a shameful family member, resign from our position, renounce our membership, or emigrate to another country. However, most often such acts of alienation (in which shame as a form of disgust felt from within morphs into disgust felt from without) are not easily accomplished, and serve, at most, only as a very last resort. Our families, vocations, religious and political commitments and memberships most often define us to the extent that renouncing them amounts to some extent to self-denial. Condemning the conduct, policies or actions of one's friends, family, religious community, longtime workplace or native country is one thing, walking away from them, quite another.

When dissociation is not an option, the shame we feel for being associated with the reprehensible conduct of the self-defining collectivities to which we belong is, therefore, often accompanied by a *collective* feeling of shame bred by a sense of collective responsibility and blame.[21] It is first-personal like the shame we feel *for* belonging to them, but the shame we feel *as* members of them is first-personal plural; an emotion representing a normative we-, rather than an I-judgment; a judgment that marks us off from them while remaining inside.

Bibliography

Fisch M, Benbaji Y (2011) The view from within: normativity and the limits of self-criticism. University of Notre Dame Press, South Bend

Frankfurt HG (1971) Freedom of will and the concept of a person. J Philos 67(1):5–20

Frankfurt HG (1988) The importance of what we care about: philosophical essays. Cambridge University Press, Cambridge

Frankfurt HG (2006) Taking ourselves seriously and getting it right. Stanford University Press, Stanford

Halbertal M (2007) Concealment and revelation: esotericism in Jewish thought and its philosophical implications. Princeton University Press, Princeton

Kosofsky Sedgwick E, Frank A (eds) (1995) Shame and its sisters: a Silvan Tomkins reader. Duke University Press, Durham

Nussbaum MC (2001) Upheavals of thought: the intelligence of emotions. Cambridge University Press, Cambridge

Nussbaum MC (2004) Hiding from humanity: shame, disgust, and the law. Princeton University Press, Princeton

Sartre JP (2018) Being and nothingness. Routledge, Abingdon

Taylor C (1985a) Human agency and language: philosophical papers, vol I. Cambridge University Press, Cambridge

Taylor G (1985b) Pride, shame and guilt. Oxford University Press, Oxford

Tuomela R (2007) The philosophy of sociality: the shared point of view. Oxford University Press, Oxford

---

[21] Although his influential notion of the "we-mode" fails to make room for the role of criticism from within a stable cohesive group, Raimo Tuomela notes emphatically that because "in the we-mode case, the group has the authority," therefore, "group members acting as group members share the authority and responsibility for whatever they do as a group" (Tuomela 2007, 56). Perhaps the most robust notion of we-mode criticism from within is Michael Walzer's notion of the connected critic, who, although Walzer does not put in terms of shame, is certainly ashamed of his community's conduct. See Walzer (1987).

Walzer M (1987) Interpretation and social criticism (The Tanner lectures on human values 1985). Harvard University Press, Cambridge, MA

Williams B (1993) Shame and necessity. University of California Press, Berkeley

Winnicott DW (1986) Holding and interpretation: fragments of an analysis. Grove Atlantic Press, New York

Chapter 4
Appreciating the Comical

Abstract The chapter sets forth from four questions any viable philosophy of humor must address: why only humans can find something funny (as opposed to pleasing or playful)? Why what they find funny is limited to their world? Why is finding something funny the only feat of understanding that is rewarded by an animalistic bark of laughter? And why explaining a joke spoils it? Several theories of humor are briefly examined and rejected in favor of an updated version of Schopenhauer's so-called "incongruity' approach.

Keywords Amusement · Ruining a joke · Superiority theories · Relief theories · Incongruity theories · Freud · Henri Bergson · Arthur Schopehauer · Conceptual language · Rationality

Like shame, amusement, namely, the ability to enjoy the comic and the humorous, is also an exclusively human emotion. However, it might seem quite out of place in the present work alongside shame and humility. For unlike humility and the quintessential forms of shame we have discussed, enjoying a joke would seem not to be a reflexive response at all, except for the rare cases in which we find ourselves to be funny. However, from the perspective developed in what follows I shall argue (taking my cue from Schopenhauer) that, despite being rarely self-directed, our very ability to appreciate the comic harbors a profound and inherent reflexivity that, no less than shame, and humility, goes to the very heart of what makes us human.

© The Author(s), under exclusive license to Springer Nature
Switzerland AG 2025
M. Fisch, *Reflexive Emotions*, SpringerBriefs in Philosophy,
https://doi.org/10.1007/978-3-031-83764-7_4

4.1 Humor's Double Nature

Let me start with a true, yet in all probability fictitious anecdote concerning the late Rabbi Joseph B. Soloveitchik, leading North American religious leader and Jewish thinker. At one of his famous, well-attended Saturday-night lectures, so the story goes, he found himself rudely and repeatedly interrupted by two snickering yeshiva lads of a rival denomination. The Rabbi is reputed to have responded by telling them to: "please make an effort to understand the lesson, if you are unable to do so, please try to restrain yourselves, and if you are unable to do that, then by all means keep laughing, because that is the only way we'll know you are human." The capacities that enable us to follow a complicated presentation, to hold our impulses and desires in normative check and to find something funny, are all exclusively human. However, like many, Soloveitchik seems to have considered humor the lowest of the three. The thesis of humor's relative inferiority has a long history, to which I shall return shortly. But first to what sharply distinguishes humor from the other, supposedly superior two—human understanding and normative restraint.

First, unlike human understanding and self-restraint, for which one finds considerable rudimentary antecedents in other animals, our capacity to find something amusing (as opposed to finding it pleasing, enjoyable, or even playful) seems to be exclusively human and wholly unanticipated in animal kingdom.

Second, as Henri Bergson acutely observed, appreciation of the comic is not only an exclusive human *capacity*, but what humans consider funny

> does not exist outside the pale of what is strictly human. A landscape may be beautiful, charming and sublime, or insignificant and ugly; it will never be laughable. You may laugh at an animal, but only because you have detected in it some human attitude or expression.[1]

Only humans can appreciate a joke, and what they find funny has always to do with their world.

Third, although getting a joke and finding something funny is an exclusively human accomplishment that requires an informed, insider's grasp of the relevant human context, no other feat of human understanding comes accompanied by anything even remotely analogous to the animal bark of laughter at finding something funny, that seems to issue forth from the depths of our pre-human animal nature, with a force capable at times of causing momentary incontinence. Involuntary and uncontrollable peals of laughter are akin to similarly animalistic howls of pain and wails of sorrow. But while the latter two have clear parallels in the animal world, the

---

[1] Bergson (2014, 3). An interesting example is the erotic revue "Oh! Calcutta!" that comprised several musical dance numbers intercepted by humorous skits of an erotic nature. The former were sung and danced in the nude, but for the latter the actors had to be clothed, if only minimally. Similar to there being no such thing as a peeping Tom in a nudist colony, it turned out to be impossible to perform a rowdy, sexy skit buck naked; impossible to joke about sex au naturel with no human sexual taboo to break!

4.1 Humor's Double Nature

former has none. Laughter is a decidedly pre-human component of a decidedly and exclusively human experience.

Fourth and last, getting a joke is an accomplishment rewarded by laughter, but unlike any other cognitive achievement, a joke is irredeemably ruined by explaining it. Nothing is spoilt when a painting, a piece of music, a philosophical argument or a mathematical proof are explained to us. On the contrary, when well explained we often feel enlightened and enjoy an elevated sense of enriched comprehension. A well explained work of art or philosophical argument can be better appreciated and enjoyed, yet the one sure way to spoil a joke is to explain why it's funny!

What exactly is spoilt when a joke or comical situation is explained? What sort of cognitive achievement is involved in finding something funny? And what exactly does a burst of laughter at a good joke express? I doubt that a convincing philosophical explanation of the nature of the comical and our gleeful reaction to it can spoil them for us as does explaining a joke. Still, philosophy, especially of the analytical variety, can be a serious fun spoiler. The late Israeli philosopher Eddy Zemach once told me how the guests at a gathering he attended at Oxford decided to play a party game in which everyone was required to choose an adverb or adjective—angrily, dubiously, joyfully, etc.—act accordingly throughout the evening, and at midnight try to guess each other's choice of word. Being the only philosopher in the room, Zemach told me, he chose to act "philosophically", and spent the evening asking people to define their terms, prompting them to clarify their remarks, and so forth. At midnight there was a wall-to-wall consensus that he had chosen "boringly". He was so embarrassed, he said, that he declared them right...

Humor has a long history of being looked down upon as an inferior form of human expression for its shallow frivolity and unseriousness in comparison to loftier forms of human reasoning and contemplation, in relation to which laughter is not merely deemed lower but detrimental. Plato and Aristotle condemned it as such.[2] Rabbi Soloveitchik' s reputed cynical response to his snickering hecklers clearly echoes the same sentiment, which is immortalized in the role assigned to Aristotle's lost work on comedy in the murderous plot of Umberto Eco's *The Name of Rose*. However, such deemings of humor's inferior repute, even if valid, have, of themselves, little to offer by way of answering any of the four questions raised above concerning the exclusively human, yet curiously split nature of the comical: Why can only humans enjoy the comical? Why is what they find funny always related human life? Why does getting a joke come accompanied by a bark a laughter, and what does it express? And why does explaining a joke spoil it?

---

[2] For Plato see *Republic* Bk.3, 388c-388d, for Aristotle, e.g. *Ethics*, iv, 8.

4.2 Theories of the Comical

It is customary to group philosophical and psychological explanatory accounts of humor under three main headings.[3] The first, classifies finding something amusing as a form of judgment of others; the second, as an essentially bodily release of energy; the third, as responding to the particular structure of the comical.

So-called *superiority theories* see it as a form of scornful aggression levelled deridingly in mockery of others or of one's former self. Such accounts view laughter as a muted, defensive version of ferocious teeth-baring directed against fellow humans and their worlds—which at once nicely accounts for humor's double nature and succeeds in making evolutionary sense of it as a less singularly human phenomenon. But it is considerably less successful in explaining why explaining a joke spoils it. In arguing in favor of a cognitivist approach to the emotions, Nussbaum makes much of the fact that contrary to moods and sensations like weariness, stomach cramps and dizziness, emotional responses can be reasoned with.[4] New evidence and new explanations of known evidence can ease or deepen a person's grief and anxiety, and dampen or intensify her delight and disgust.

Yet making explicit the crucial data needed to appreciate a joke doesn't seem to have the same effect on levels of amusement. If what one's supposed to find funny boils down in the last analysis to boundary-marking assertions of his or her relative superiority in relation to others, then all jokes are essentially insider jokes. Not getting a joke can, therefore, owe to one of two: either because not getting it reveals one not to be an insider, in which case explaining it would be pointless, or because though an insider, one lacks the relevant knowledge regarding those being laughed at. Peter Berger offers the following as an example of humor's "boundary-marking" function. A young Jewish social worker working out west on a reservation, falls in love and marries a Native-American girl, whom he eventually takes back to New York City. After a year she comes home for a visit.

> "Are you happy?" her folks ask her.
> "Oh, yes, very happy."
> "Is he treating you right?"
> "Oh yes, he is just great."
> "And what about his family? We've been told that Jews don't much like it if their children marry outsiders. How does his family feel about their son marrying an Indian girl?"
> "Oh fine. They've been wonderful to me. They've even given me a new name. They call me Sitting Shiva."[5]

No one with any acquaintance with Jewish custom would miss the irony of the name. But one can easily imagine American ultraorthodox, and very many

---

[3] For a useful summary see the Stanford Encyclopedia entry on the Philosophy of humor: https://plato.stanford.edu/entries/humor/ accessed March 18, 2021.

[4] e.g. Nussbaum (2001, 46–47).

[5] Berger (2014, 54).

4.2 Theories of the Comical

non-American Jews sufficiently unacquainted with Native-American lore, who would completely miss the joke's 'Sitting Bull' allusion. Filling them in on the information they lack would allow them to get the joke's point. They might better understand why those who laugh at it find it funny, but it is doubtful that they themselves would now be tickled by it after the event.

There seems to be an immediacy about how we react to humor, which, unlike other emotions, renders it largely immune to retroactive enlightenment. Discovering new information or achieving better understanding of a situation can significantly intensify or diminish our initial emotional response to it, but the glee aroused by a joke or a comical state-of-affairs doesn't seem to work that way. The familiar image of the grim-faced pedant laughing at a joke hours later after finally getting it is comical in ways that seeing the way out a riddle, or when the significance of something we saw, heard or read dawns on us long after the event, does not. Superiority accounts of humor are of no help in this regard.

The identification of the comical with ridicule and scornful mockery has firm roots in both the Bible and Greek philosophy. In response to "the Kings of the earth" who "set themselves ... against the Lord and his anointed", states the Psalmist

> He that sitteth in the heavens shall laugh: the LORD shall have them in derision. Then shall he speak unto them in his wrath, and vex them in his sore displeasure.[6]

This is as close as one gets to a biblical definition of (divine) laughter as holding the subjects of His humor in wrathful derision. The Greek case would appear to be similar, given the highly significant role assigned to the comedies in Athenian democracy. From at least the late 480's BC onwards, the tragedy and comedy competitions constituted the highlights of the festive City Dionysia. The tragedies' somber and sobering reflections on human nature, religion and politics were highly valued, but it was the comedies' rude unruly fun-poking ridicule, aimed devastatingly at the city's life, institutions, high culture and leadership, that proved the most popular and the most effective. Their role in provoking self-critique by derision was indispensable.[7] In both Plato and Aristotle the laughable is identified with the ridiculous. And "What is ridiculous in Greek culture in general... [and] in Plato in particular," argues Naas, "is thus what is worthless or meaningless, ugly or unattractive, lowly, vile and shameful."[8]

However, although humor can be, and certainly is widely *employed* with a view (consciously or unconsciously) to scorn, ridicule, jeer, and mock, still, much of what we find funny seems not to fall in that category at all. Unlike political satire and comedians poking fun across dividing gender, ethnic, cultural and socially related lines, jokes like the following—another *shiva* joke—are all-pervasive. It's a Jewish gallows tale about an elderly married couple, which is no way particularly

---

[6] Psalms 2: 4–5, (KJV). The Jerusalem Bible's version is truer to the Hebrew: "He who sits in heavens laughs: The Lord has them in derision. Then shall he speak to them in his wrath, and terrify them in his burning anger."

[7] Goldhill (1987).

[8] Nass (2016, 20).

34 4 Appreciating the Comical

Jewish. It tells of an ailing old man, who hears his wife knocking about in the kitchen.

"What are you making, love?", he asks in a weak voice.
"An apple strudel", she calls back.
"Oh I love apple strudel, could I have a piece", he croaks.
"No, love, it's for the *shiva*", she answers.

Replace "*shiva*" with "wake" or "*mansaf*"[9] and nothing changes. It's a good, if somewhat cruel joke that mocks no one, and marks no social boundaries. Humor undoubtedly plays a major role in the service of human expressions of mock and scornful critique, grave and mild, but that is a far cry from claiming with arch-superiority theorist, Thomas Hobbes, "that the passion of laughter is *nothing else but* sudden glory arising from some sudden conception of some eminency in ourselves, by comparison with the infirmity of others, or with our own formerly".[10]

Unlike superiority theories that aspire to characterize humor as an attitudinal form of judgment, the so-called *relief theories* of the comic portray finding something funny not in terms of what the joke purports to say or to express, or the funny situation, to convey, but in terms of the tension-relief, as they deem it, granted by laughter itself. Humor, they claim, acts as a release valve for pent up nervous (or in Freud's case, psychic) energy. According to relief theorists, to laugh is to perform a bodily function whose function is to let off steam. Herbert Spencer, the first major proponent of the relief theory tellingly entitled his essay "The Physiology of Laughter".[11] Freud's tripartite theory of the three sources of laughter—joking, the comic, and humor—follows suit in viewing them as serving to discharge by laughter different forms of pent up unusable psychic energy[12]: joking, according to Freud, builds up an excess of energy used to stifle feelings that is released in laughter, the comic builds up cognitive, and the humorous, emotional surpluses of energy, which are then expended by laughing.

However, insofar as the very amusement experienced when we find something funny is indeed an emotion, relief theories have very little to offer. Even if they do regard laughter as an emotional response, deeming it to be purely physiological, is to cast that emotion squarely in non-cognitivist terms, and consequently beyond the pale of the present study's concerns.[13] More importantly, it fails to explain any of humor's four prominent features mentioned above: why only humans can find something funny? Why is what they find funny wholly limited to the human world? Why getting a joke is the only feat of human comprehension that comes

---

[9] For the wide variety of funerary ritual meals see Yoder (1986) and references there.

[10] Hobbes (1812, ch.9, §13) (italics added).

[11] Spencer (1860).

[12] Freud (2003, 142–146).

[13] Spencer viewed laughter as paradigmatic of emotion in general. "laughter is a display of muscular excitement," he writes, "and so illustrates the general law, that feeling passing a certain pitch habitually vents itself in bodily action" (1860, 398).

accompanied by a hard to control physical reaction? And why does explaining a joke spoil it?

4.3 Two Incongruity Theories

In this regard, *incongruity theories* of humor fair better than the other two. Jokes and other situations we find funny, they claim, share a basic split structure. In what is usually referred to as the "setup" of a joke or comic situation an expectation is formed, which in a sudden twist or turn of events, is radically transformed "into nothing", as Kant puts it in the Third Critique, by means of an unexpected "punch line".[14] The comical in all its forms certainly builds on such a kind of rude and surprising elimination of a firm expectation, as in the joke cited by Kant of the well-to-do heir who sought to arrange a grand funeral for a relative, only to find that the more he paid his mourners, the happier they became!

But why do we find this funny? Many surprising denials of expectation can be deeply disturbing. Most incongruity theories fail to explain which surprising turns of events tickle us, and why? I would like to look at two interestingly contradicting incongruity accounts of the comical—those of Bergson and Schopenhauer—that both go that extra step, and do so with a view to siding with the latter.

4.3.1 Henri Bergson

For Bergson laughter expresses a triumph of the intelligence. "The comic," he writes,

> will come into being… whenever a group of men concentrate their attention on one of their number, imposing silence on their emotions and calling into play nothing but their intelligence.[15]

The flexibility and adaptability of the human intellect is what ensures the vitality of human life. Its arch-enemy is hence the rigid, mechanical, preconditioned, and unthinking modes of being and responding that treat the new as mere repetitions of the old. According to Bergson, the inherent incongruity at the heart of everything we find funny is that between an expectation born of habit, attributed to the subject of the joke or created in the mind of its addressee, and the reality that flies in its face, which we realize in retrospect required being assessed anew. Humor confronts our mechanical, instinctive, merely physiological selves—ourselves, as Bergson has it, as mere *things* (*ibid*)—with ourselves as active, pliant, and supplely responsive intellects. To get a joke is to realize reason's superiority over instinct, however well-tuned; of intellect over nature (and we might add: especially over second-nature).

---

[14] Kant (2019, 160–162).
[15] Bergson (2014, 8).

Laughter expresses reason's gleeful triumph. So, as many have noted, Bergson's incongruity theory contains an interesting "superiority" component, but one that has nothing to do with ethnic or cultural superiority, with deriding others, or with social boundary control. It is not at all about feeling superior to other people or groups, but about the superiority of our reason over our instinct; of keeping an open and flexible mind over responding by rote. As such, it understands the glee and amusement expressed in laughter as an inherently *reflexive* emotion. What it explains less well is the nature of laughter itself. If what is enjoyed in a joke is the triumph of reason, laughter's animalistic, uncontrollable bark seems utterly out of place. We take pleasure in solving a riddle, in successfully tackling new problems that resist well-rehearsed methods, in hearing or reading about great feats of creative intellect, but none of these, even when sudden, gives rise to anything resembling a hearty guffaw.

4.3.2 Arthur Schopenhauer

The incongruity on which Schopenhauer builds his account of the ludicrous[16] is similar. It breaches an analogous divide, but is argued in exactly the opposite direction! Like Bergson, Schopenhauer too purports to offer an exhaustive theory of what Lewis (2005) nicely terms "intentional laughter", namely laughter "that is directed at something or other", as opposed to hysterical, nervous or embarrassed laughter, or laughing as a result of being tickled. But in Schopenhauer's theory, what is contrasted to reason is not human habit, but "reality"[17]; not second-nature, but nature itself, as it were. At the heart of everything we find funny, he argues, we inevitably find an "incongruity between a single real object and the concept under which …it has been rightly subsumed" (1966, vol.1, 59). The incongruity constitutive of every story, event, or state of affairs we find ludicrous (his word for funny) manifests itself between its two parts: an undisputed *major* in which an object or state of affairs is subsumed under a concept or idea,[18] and a wholly unexpected *minor* in which it is shown to fly in its face. Intentional laughter represents for Schopenhauer our gleeful response to the failure of a concept to perform its representational function.

To properly appreciate the novelty of Schopenhauer's account, a word on his theory of concepts is in order. Like all other creatures, humans are free to move in space but not in time. Like all creatures, we are firmly welded to the present moment,

---

[16] Schopenhauer discusses humor twice, first very briefly in (1966, vol.1, §13, 59–69), and in greater detail in 1966, vol.2, Ch. VIII, 91–101), entitled "On the Theory of the Ludicrous".

[17] The implied realism Schopenhauer's language with regard to the fact of experience here is irrelevant to his theory of humor. Simply replace "reality" with "reality as experienced", hence the inverted commas.

[18] Schopenhauer's distinction between concepts and ideas, his critique of Kant's treatment of the former, and (mis)interpretation of Plato's notion of the latter, all lie beyond the confines of the present work. For a clear account of all three, and the considerable literature devoted to them, see Costanzo (2020).

4.3 Two Incongruity Theories

totally immobile, unable to budge forward or back in time or even remain stationary as time ticks on. Forever rooted in the present, we are endowed, as are all other living creatures, with sense organs that allow us to take in and appreciate the rich, kaleidoscopic sensuous dazzle of the here and the now.

However, unlike any other creature, humankind has found a way to revisit the past and envisage the future without having to move in time that enables us to learn the lessons of yesterday and plan for tomorrow. We do so by means of the unique conceptual languages at our disposal. Concepts like dog, person, parent, and promise allow us to travel in time, as it were, recalling, and learning from past experience, making sense of present happenings, and anticipating or planning for those to come. While other animals—our "irrational brothers", as Schopenhauer calls them—live in the present, man alone

> lives at the same time in the future and the past. They satisfy the need of the moment; he provides by the most ingenious preparations for his future, nay, even for times that he cannot live to see. They are given up entirely to the impression of the moment...; he is determined by abstract concepts independent of the present moment. He therefore carries out considered plans, or acts in accordance with maxims, without regard to his surroundings, and to the accidental impressions of the moment (vol.1, §8, 36).

However, argues Schopenhauer, our conceptual ability's great payoff comes at a very steep price. In order to perform their trans-temporal role and remain true to the endless time-bound realities they purport to represent, the designata of concepts like dog, person and promise are necessarily limited to what all dogs, all people and all promises have respectively in common.[19] At every level, concepts are inevitably generic; flattened abstract schemata capable of transcending the here and the now only at the price of systematically erasing everything that renders any particular dog, person or promise, unique (as he remarked of his beloved poodle Atma).

Though faithful to Kant's distinction, Schopenhauer drives a wedge between human sentience and sapience, between reason and intuition (in Kant's sense of the term). We reason, by means of concepts, yet experience our world with an unmediated sensual immediacy that, in its particularity, richness, and resolution, defies full conceptualization by definition. He profoundly reverses Plato's famous cave allegory. If Plato likens what we perceive to mere distortive shadows of the ideal forms we are capable of conceiving, Schopenhauer likens the objects of reason to the merely reflected light of the moon, giving the term "reflection" an intriguing and ironic twist.

> As from the direct light of the sun to the borrowed reflected light of the moon, so do we pass from the immediate representation of perception, which stands by itself and is its own warrant, to reflection, to the abstract, discursive concepts of reason (*vernunft*), which have their whole content only from that knowledge of perception and in relation to it. (vol.1, §8, 35)

And yet, "rational knowledge, the application of reason" by means of concepts can never fully comprehend "knowledge of perception" in all its particular richness.

---

[19] Whether one views concepts as generalizing over groups, or designating exemplars (see ch.1 n.9 above), Schopenhauer's distinction holds.

"Concepts, with their rigidity and sharp delineation, however finely they may be split by closer definition, are forever incapable of reaching the fine modifications of perception" (vol.1, §12, 56–57) "Reason is necessary," Schopenhauer submits,

> in the high stress of life where rapid decisions, bold action, quick and firm comprehension are needed, but if it gains the upper hand, if it confuses and hinders the intuitive, immediate discovery of what is right by the pure understanding, and at the same time prevents this from being grasped, and if it produces irresolution, then it can easily ruin everything. (57-58)

According to Schopenhauer, it is this essential incongruity between conceiving and perceiving, between reason and the reality to which its concepts are applied, that lies at the heart of everything we find funny. "In everything that excites laughter" it is always possible to show

> a concept and a particular, that is to say, a thing or an event, which can of course be subsumed under that concept, and thus be thought through it, yet which in another and predominating respect does not belong under it at all, but differs strikingly from everything else thought through that concept. (1966, vol.2, ch.8, 91-92)

Two of his examples drive the point home nicely. That of the epigram describing the deadeningly boring preacher as:

> Bav is the true shepherd of whom the Bible spake:
>   If his flock be asleep, he alone remains awake,

And that describing the negligent dead physician who like a hero now lies, "and those he has slain lie around him" (vol.2, 93).

But it is not the mere incongruity "between what is conceived and what is perceived" (98), nor the sheer suddenness of its realization that makes us laugh. What we rejoice and find pleasure in (typically cast by the misogynic Schopenhauer in feminine terms) is "to see this strict, untiring, and most troublesome governess, our faculty of reason, for once convicted of inadequacy" (98). The reason, Schopenhauer explains, is that whenever a contrast suddenly appears

> between the perceived and the conceived, the perceived is always undoubtedly in the right, for it is in no way subject to error, and needs no confirmation from outside, but is its own advocate. Its conflict with what is thought springs ultimately from the fact that the latter, with its abstract concepts, cannot come down to the infinite multifariousness and fine shades of what is perceived. This triumph of knowledge of perception over thought gives us pleasure. (98)

And it is a pleasure, Schopenhauer insists, that runs deep. Not grounded, or not properly confirmed by perception, conceptual knowledge remains abstract, empty and misleading. Books do not take the place of experience, because *concepts* always remain *universal,* and, therefore, can never fully reach down to the particular. Yet it is precisely the particular that has to be dealt with in life. It follows that all the great woes and calamities that plague human life ultimately owe to the inherent, built-in inadequacies of our conceptual vocabularies, without which there could not be human life to begin with, but which bestow upon it an inevitable schematic shortsightedness.

4.4 Schopenhauer and Beyond

While in real life reason's inherent shortcomings can prove hazardous, in humorous situations we are never at risk (unless we are the subject of the jest). What we experience with dumbfounding abruptness each time we find something funny, is a significant, yet at the same time unthreatening conceptual failure on our part. It is not the mere incongruity between our perceptual and conceptual knowledge that tickles us, according to Schopenhauer, but the fact that the latter is so thoroughly trumped by the former! Moreover it is an incongruity we perceive with all the immediacy of our perceptual ability, rather than think about or brood on it. That is why, I believe, explaining a joke so thoroughly spoils it!

But Schopenhauer's main point is that the emotion expressed in laughing is a special kind of delight. We are not merely privy to being privy to two categorically different forms of knowledge. Our perceptual and conceptual knowledge are acquired by means of two related yet quite distinct subsystems—one we share with all other animals, and one that sets us apart from every other animal. We are especially proud of our rationality and speech. For one thing, it is only by means of our ability to think and to speak that the very distinction between the two epistemic realms can be made. And yet, it is our thinking and speaking that are kept in check by our perceiving, and when not, they run the risk of gravely misleading us. Our rational nature, aloof and always distant, looks down at our sensual animal nature as base and ill-defined, callous and lacking of real meaning, despite being always at its mercy. But every time we laugh, according to Schopenhauer, it is at our rational self's expense!

And it is more than mere aloofness. Because all speech and thought depends on them, our concepts' inherent limitations have enjoyed a long history of delusionary platonic apologetics, as if the low, drastically flattening common denominator shared by all creatures conceived as dogs, captures their very essence, their very informing form, rendering secondary and accidental and, therefore, inconsequential, everything that makes each one of them special and different; as if what different things are thought to share is more real than they themselves...

4.4 Schopenhauer and Beyond

Schopenhauer's account belongs squarely among the so-called incongruity theories of the comic, but, like that of Bergson, it also combines a unique and equally essential element of superiority. And just like Bergson's account, so here the superiority expressed each time we laugh at something is self-directed, rather than directed at the subject of the joke, or at other people. Getting a joke is indeed a cognitive feat only our rational self can perform. To appreciate the incongruity a joke embodies, one must be well-acquainted with its relevant context and the concepts in which it is cast. Yet contrary to Bergson, according to Schopenhauer, it is not our rational self who is amused when we laugh, for the joke, as it were, is always on it! Whenever we find something funny, the part of us enjoying itself and given to fits of laughter is without exception, in Schopenhauer's view, the perceptive, sensual self we share

40   4 Appreciating the Comical

with the rest of animal kingdom. No wonder then that getting a good joke comes accompanied by such a primordial, pre-rational bark of laughter or uncontrollable giggle. It is the sound of the animal within us, getting the best of its haughty yet failed rational counterpart, thoroughly enjoying itself at its expense.[20]

Schopenhauer's account fares better than any other we have looked at so far, with respect to the four questions with which we set forth: namely, why only humans are able to enjoy a joke? Why what they are liable to find funny is restricted to their world? Why unlike any other feat of the understanding getting a good joke is rewarded by an animalistic chortle? And why explaining a joke spoils it?

But in one important respect Schopenhauer's theory is seriously out of date. The days in which philosophers equated human rationality with the ability to achieve and vouch for certitude, to transcend mere *doxa* and boast ascertained *episteme*, to construct our picture of the world by the power of our thought, as Descartes believed we could, or by inferring up from empirical data, with absolute, timeless certainty, are long gone. Cast in Popperian terms, or from the more subtle and challenging neo-Kantian perspectives of Thomas Kuhn and his followers in philosophy of science,[21] or Sellars and Rorty and their followers in philosophy of mind,[22] human rationality is perceived not only as fallible, but as humbly aware of its fallibility. As we shall see in greater detail in the following chapter, agents at their very rational best combine a humble awareness of their liability to err, as Popper unremittingly insisted, with an equally insistent awareness of the inherent limits of *self*-criticism, and, hence, of their need for critical input from without (a point wholly overlooked by Popper).

From such a perspective, *because* rational, our rational self will never view failures of concept application as failures of rationality, but as part and parcel of an ongoing and highly rational process of learning from its mistakes. While the animal within us revels in its perceptual superiority each time we enjoy a good joke, our rational self, well aware of the inherent limitations and inevitable shortsightedness of our diverse conceptual schemes it cannot do without, enjoys an astounding moment, not of unwitting humiliating defeat, but of humble enlightened realization. Laughter thus emerges as a *co-produced* reaction, essentially combining both cognitive and non-cognitive elements. From our animal self's perspective, it is a howl

---

[20] Although Schopenhauer's philosophy is widely characterized as pessimistic—famously since Copleston (1975)—few discuss his account of humor in this context. For an interesting exception see Lewis (2005).

[21] For an insightful survey of Kuhn's immediate neo-Kantian background in the works of Moritz Schlick, Hans Reichenbach and Rudolph Carnap, a critical assessment of Kuhn's *Structure*, and an interesting attempt to go beyond it, see Michael Friedman (2001). For a critique of Friedman, and an alternative neo-Kantian account of the rationality scientific framework transitions see Fisch (2017).

[22] See especially Sellars (1957), Rorty (1989, chs.1–3), McDowell (1994), Brandom (2009, Part. I), Taylor C. (1985, chs.1,2 & 4), and Fisch and Benbaji (2011, chs.1, 6–8).

or bark of delight in the face of an inarticulable[23] triumph, but from that of our rational self it is a self-directed emotional response in the best of the cognitivist tradition: a mixture of amusement at being cleverly caught out, and the joy of realizing something new that would never had occurred to it otherwise. And thus, I suggest, building on and away from Schopenhauer, what makes humor so special is how the profoundly incongruous, uniquely human coupling of body and mind, perception and reason, animal and rational is transformed, in a highly enjoyable, perceptive yet unthreatening flash, into a whole that is not merely larger than its two incongruous parts, but whose parts prove and realize to their sheer delight how their fruitful co-dependence and critical cooperation renders us human.

Bibliography

Berger PL (2014) Redeeming laughter: the comic dimension of human experience, 2nd edn. De Gruyter, Berlin
Bergson H (2014) Laughter: an essay on the meaning of the comic. Martino Fine Books, Eastford
Brandom RB (2009) Reason in philosophy: animating ideas. Harvard University Press, Cambridge, MA
Copleston FC (1975) Arthur Schopenhauer philosopher of pessimism. Barnes & Noble Books, New York
Costanzo J (2020) Schopenhauer's interpretation of the platonic ideas. The International Journal of the Platonic Tradition 14:153–175
Fisch M (2017) Creatively undecided: toward a history and philosophy of scientific agency. University of Chicago Press, Chicago
Fisch M, Benbaji Y (2011) The view from within: normativity and the limits of self-criticism. University of Notre Dame Press, South Bend
Freidman M (2001) Dynamics of reason. CSLI Publications, Stanford
Freud S (2003) The joke and its relation to the unconscious (trans: Crick J, with introduction by John Carey). Penguin Books, London
Goldhill SD (1987) The Great Dionysia and civic ideology. J Hell Stud 107(1):58–76
Hobbes T (1812) The treatise on human nature, and that on liberty and necessity with a supplement. J. Johnson and Co., London
Kant I (2019) Critique of Judgment (trans: Bernard JH). Digireads Publishing, Overland Park
Lewis PB (2005) Schopenhauer's Laughter. Monist 88(1):36–51
McDowell J (1994) Mind and world. Harvard University Press, Cambridge, MA
Nass M (2016) Plato and the spectacle of laughter. Angelaki J Theor Humanit 21(3):13–26
Nussbaum MC (2001) Upheavals of thought: the intelligence of emotions. Cambridge University Press, Cambridge
Rorty R (1989) Contingency, irony, solidarity. Cambridge University Press, Cambridge

---

[23] Schopenhauer makes much of the fact that our perceptual knowledge is of itself inarticulable:

Actually all truth and all wisdom ultimately lie in *perception;* but unfortunately perception cannot be either retained or communicated. ... Only the poorest knowledge, abstract secondary knowledge, the concept, the mere shadow of knowledge proper, is unconditionally communicable (1966, vol.2, ch.7, 74).

Schopenhauer A (1966) The world as will and representation (trans: Payne EFJ, 2 vols). Dover Publications, Mineola

Sellars W (1957) Empiricism and the philosophy of mind. Minn Stud Philos Sci 1(19):253–329

Spencer H (1860) The physiology of laughter. Macmillan's Magazine 1:395–402

Taylor C (1985) Human agency and language: philosophical papers, vol I. Cambridge University Press, Cambridge

Yoder L (1986) The funeral meal: a significant funerary ritual. J Relig Health 25(2):149–160

Chapter 5
The Humble Self

Abstract Unlike the shame felt when failing to live up to the standards we abide by, humility is felt when prudently taking stock of, and owning up to our limitations and incapacities. If shame motivates self-correction, humility motivates outsourcing to others, better equipped or positioned for the task at hand. In this sense humility is shown to be an inherent component of rational action. However, the chapter goes on to argue, owning up to our inability in principle of holding our normative commitments themselves in normative check, and realizing the crucial importance of being criticized by others in this regard, renders this form of humble outsourcing the very epitome of rationality.

Keywords Humility · Rationality · Self-criticism · Robert Brandom · The reasons game · Second-order volitions · I-part · Normative self-critique · External criticism · Normative ambivalence

5.1 Introduction: Humility as Emotion

Humility belongs alongside shame and humor not only because it is perhaps the most reflexive of emotions, but because like shame and humor—and contrary, for example, to pride—it is also decidedly and constructively self-critical—an observation that will acquire an interesting twist as we go forward. Self-criticism can be an enriching motivating force for self-correction, but it can also have the opposite effect. For people who hold themselves accountable to unrealizable standards, self-critique can be crippling and can lead to incapacitating self-despair. This is certainly true of shame. Secondary shame in particular, as we have seen, can act as a powerful normative restraint and self-corrective, but, as Martha Nussbaum's work shows, can be pathologically guilt-ridden and self-defeating. Humor is different. It is impossible to imagine finding something so funny as to render our rational self

© The Author(s), under exclusive license to Springer Nature
Switzerland AG 2025
M. Fisch, *Reflexive Emotions*, SpringerBriefs in Philosophy,
https://doi.org/10.1007/978-3-031-83764-7_5

dumbfounded to the point of despair.[1] Humility is more like shame in this regard, but quite unlike shame, of itself, even when unfounded in the extreme, humility can incapacitate, but rarely breeds guilt.

Even more than shame and shaming, humility and humiliation have little to do with one another. Neither causes the other. One can be profoundly humble yet not feel in the least humiliated, and be cruelly humiliated without feeling at all humbled. Unlike shame, humility is not a response to the defilement of one's inner self by intrusive others, nor does it express guilt or self-blame for failing to live up to standards to which one holds oneself accountable. Humility is the emotional uptake of candid self-assessment and sober awareness of one's limits and incapacities. It builds on a form of self-evaluation, which, although usually lacking an element of self-rebuke, frequently motivates taking corrective action, though less frequently in the form of *self*-improvement, except, of course, when deemed mistaken or unjustifiably ill-prepared. Knowing one's limitations requires leaving, delegating and outsourcing action and responsibility to those one considers better positioned or better capable of taking or assuming it.

Like other forms of judgment, emotions can remain 'theoretical' or lead to the emotive equivalent of practical reasoning. Fear, pity, compassion and joy are at times merely felt, but at other times motivate acting, even urgently—freezing, hiding or fleeing in the case of fear, assisting or comforting in the case of pity, and so forth. Humility is no different. At times, honestly owning up to our shortcomings will cause us to merely feel humble, but at other times will motivate us, when required, to compensate for them by seeking assistance, expert opinion, and so forth. Humility can also serve as a powerful incentive for *in*action, for keeping our thoughts to ourselves, for leaving to others what we believe needs to be done, or resolving to be better prepared in the future.

Although frequently taken to be synonymous,[2] humility is different from modesty. Modesty is more of a disposition toward others than a form of self-judgment. A modest person may be fully aware of her capabilities, advantages and strengths, but prefer not to flaunt them. Modesty, even if considered an emotion, is not reflexive. Humility, if genuine, is wholly reflexive. It is not about concealing or revealing one's strengths, assets, or weaknesses, but first and foremost, about *owning up* to them *to oneself*.[3] These can be misjudged and unfoundedly overrated, of course, leading, when overrated, to excessive meekness, docility, compliance and timidity, and to even more extreme forms of self-effacement (as is the case in several religious traditions where the mega-virtue of total submission is made to rest on the

---

[1] Joking at someone else's expense with a view to ridicule and shame can certainly have an unfounded, crippling effect on the victim's self-esteem. But that is where joking ceases to be funny, and morphs into ridicule, bullying and plain shaming.

[2] See, for instance Kellenberger (2010), especially pp. 322–328, and references there.

[3] For a pertinent account of intellectual humility in terms of self-owning-up see Whitcomb et al. (2017).

5.1 Introduction: Humility as Emotion

self-negating acknowledgment of divine perfection[4]). They can also be misjudged and underplayed in the opposite direction, giving rise to equally unfounded vain overconfidence that harbors its own pathologies. But a little more needs to be said about humility proper before we can properly turn our attention to how it is liable to go wrong.

Treating humility as an emotion, as a form of spontaneous reflexive judgment—as opposed to a virtue, a disposition, or a mere character trait, to which the lion's share of the literature on humility is devoted—highlights its self-evaluative nature, and its role in motivating corrective action, which, as noted, unlike secondary shame, it largely performs uncondemningly, and hence without resource to feelings of anger, self- discontent, guilt or shame. It prompts a different form of correction. In the ideal case, secondary shame motivates self-correction. When ashamed, we admonish ourselves for our normative failing, and resolve to do our best not to allow our unwanted desires and impulses to get the better of us in the future. In secondary shame, normative critique breeds a desire for tighter normative self-control and resolve to self-improve. Humility is different in this regard. It passes judgment, not on our failure, but on our *inability* to meet standards to which we abide. Ideally, therefore, Humility does not hold us accountable or blame us for not living up to them. Candidly owning up to our limitations creates level-headed critical distance between who we are and who we'd perhaps like to have been, but fall short of being; between what we are capable of and have a capacity for, and what we do not. Genuine humility transforms such self-critical assessments into two types of reasoned resolve, one negative one positive.

As noted, humility is first and foremost a guide to *in*action. The truly humble know when to step down and refrain from overstepping their capacities; when not to voice an opinion, when not to act even when there's reason to. To act rationally is to act for a reason; to intervene when something is sufficiently amiss to merit intervening—more on this immediately. But rationality does not stop there. Even if it is plainly apparent that someone requires urgent medical attention, or the aircraft we are about to fly on, urgent pre-flight testing, it would be rashly irrational for me to undertake these tasks! Rationality requires one to determine not only which action needs to be taken, but whether he or she are the right persons for the job. And this leads, of course, to the two immediate types of *positive* rational action humility motivates: outsourcing to others tasks we deem them to be better suited, positioned, or endowed to perform than ourselves, and, of course, where appropriate, self-improvement, as when one resolves to take a first-aid or self-defense course so as not to be caught off guard the next time.

As we shall see in a moment, the intimate connection between rationality and humility runs deeper still. However, enough has already been said to suggest that just as primary shame goes to the heart of human selfhood, secondary shame, to our very normativity, and humor, to the foundations of human language and reason, so

---

[4] Many of the large number of religiously motivated books on the virtues of human humility before God, can be summarized by the title of Murray (2013): *Humility & Absolute Surrender*.

humility goes to heart of human rationality. And it is to this thought that I devote the following pages.

5.2 Rationality and Critique

The first thing to notice is that regardless of the role humility plays *in* acting rationally, humility is, in, and of itself, a form *of* rational conduct, albeit spontaneous. As in former work, the approach to rationality adopted here stands in firm opposition to decision- and especially game-theoretical accounts. To the former, because not all rational action is reducible to deliberating alternatives; to the latter, because rationality cannot be exclusively identified with maximizing the actor's gain, or 'utility function.'[5] Taking my cue from the work of Sellars, McDowell, and especially Brandom, rational action is taken here to mean *premeditated* action, action taken for a reason, as opposed, not to the non-beneficial, but to what we do unthinkingly, impulsively, instinctively or involuntarily, however beneficial or desirable such activity turns out to be in retrospect. Happenings do not have to be rational to be praiseworthy. Just think of the good work your digestive and cardiovascular systems, and the autonomous areas of your brain are doing as you read these lines. It is an approach that insists that a move or act be deemed rational only when one's faculties of reason are consciously appealed to in their endorsement and performance, regardless of their actual outcome. Action can be rational on such a showing even if ultimately unsuccessful or even mistaken. Humankind is thoroughly fallible even at its rational best, and is very seldom in full control!

An act deemed rational is an act *motivated* by a reason, not merely explained by it in retrospect. What is deemed rational is hence not the actual move an actor ends up making, but *the act of agency* by means of which she deliberated, selected and endorsed the course of action she adopts. To have reason to act, to intervene in a state of affairs with a view to introducing some change in it,[6] is, first and foremost, to find it sufficiently flawed, lacking, underdeveloped, or otherwise wanting to merit such intervention. (And by the same token, to have reason not to act, is to find it preferable to its conceivable alternatives.) Here is where the profound connection between rationality and criticism first asserts itself in the simple and straightforward understanding of what it is to have initial reason to act.

---

[5] For a more detailed account of my reasons for rejecting decision- and game-theoretical accounts of rationality in favor of the approach adopted here see most recently Fisch (2025, Lecture.1, §3).

[6] This includes internal and external states of affairs. The definition thus equally straddles the distinction often made between the rationality of belief and that of action. Endorsing, jettisoning, modifying and even seriously considering a belief are all actions, which, if performed for a reason, will, according to the view presented here, be deemed rational. Not so for approaches to rationality that deem *a belief* (rather than the act of endorsing or rejecting it) to be rational when held for good reasons, or for the right reasons. See in this regard the careful distinction between reasons for a belief, and reasons for believ*ing* in Raz (2011, 19–20).

5.2 Rationality and Critique

However, the connection between rationality and criticism involves more than knowingly responding to what one deems to be in need of repair or replacement. First, as already remarked, it is not always rational for a person to intervene, even if there are good reasons to do so. If lives or fates hang in the balance, it would be wildly irrational for me to attempt to solve a problem for which I had no training, except in the most extreme circumstances. To act rationally involves, not only deeming a situation in need of repair, but acting responsibly by prudently owning up to one's relevant strengths and limitations in view of the task at hand. This alone renders humility a necessary constituent of rational conduct.

But rationality's self-directed critical component runs deeper. Just as rationality demands that we cast a wary eye around for possibly reparable flaws and failings, aware of our own failings and flaws, it requires us to be equally wary of our liability to *mis*judge such flaws and failings and the possible ways of putting them right, even when they do fall well within the purview of our capacities and responsibilities. Humility thus emerges not merely as a necessary constituent of human rationality, but of its very essence; not merely as a social virtue, or disposition toward others, but as a reflexive emotional reaction to how one stands toward oneself.

And there is more. As Sellars and especially Brandom insist, our rationality asserts itself most prominently in our willingness to engage in what they famously dub "the game of giving and asking for reasons", where, even after making our decision to act or refrain from acting and acting upon it we show keen interest in the reasons other people have for acting, and in learning what they make of ours.[7] Sellars and Brandom consider this to be the very epitome of rationality, but they nowhere explain why.[8] As we have seen, despite being *the* reflexive, self-referring emotion *par excellence*, humility's role in rationality requires being attentive to what other people are capable of where our own capacities fail us. But playing the game of giving and asking for reasons is not about outsourcing rational action to those better equipped or disposed toward taking it.

The reasons' game is played after the event. It is not about the specific action taken, so much as about exposing our reason*ing* to others and acquainting ourselves with theirs. In the terms Brandom employed in his earlier work, what we do in playing the game is to enable others to 'keep inferential score' of our commitments, of what they derive from and what they entail, to what they commit and entitle us, while allowing us to keep score of theirs. But to what end? Can humility still be at work even though we have already committed ourselves and taken the action in question? Do we ultimately engage in giving and asking others for reasons for our

---

[7] For a detailed account of his and Sellars's position on this point, see Brandom (2002, ch.12).

[8] More importantly, not only do they not explain why they consider playing the game to be rationality's high point, they nowhere attempt to explain why the game should be played in the first place. If, as they insist, we manifest our rationality most decidedly in giving and asking for reasons, the game itself *has to be* played for a reason! On this crucially important point, however, both philosophers fall inexplicably silent. For early versions of this critique and the argument presented in the following paragraphs see Fisch and Benbaji (2011, 179–184)

interlocutors' critique or their reassurance? Do we play the game as an external extension of our humility, or with a view to overcoming it?

The answer might seem obvious. Who knows one better than oneself? Who is, therefore, in a better position to prudently awake to and expose our limitations and weaknesses than we are? Self-critique, many would claim, is forever better informed and when prudent more effectively focused than any external variety. On the other hand external reassurance can help us build and regain our confidence far better than we can ever hope to achieve by talking to ourselves.[9] But as far as criticism is concerned, the opposite is true. To see why, two further point need to be made.

5.3 Humility's Dialectic and the Split Self

As argued at the outset of this work, treating humility as an emotion is to view it as a form of personal judgment. Not all emotions are reflexive, but they all represent personal appraisals of objects or states of affairs, internal or external that bear on what we value. Our emotional responses epitomize how we gauge ourselves and our world in terms of what we hold important, the things that anger and frighten us, those that sadden us and make us happy, what we are ashamed of, love, find funny, rejoice in, are disgusted by, admire, grieve, and more. As noted further, these also include our exclusively human emotional responses to our emotional responses, as when we detest our rejoicing in someone's downfall, when we fume at injustice and are proud of our reaction, fear our anxiety or are ashamed of our disgust. Emotional responses are spontaneous, resolute, and not in the least hesitant. Emotional judgment is passed and acted on assertively. Our emotional reactions are liable to be proven wrong, of course, both in misperceiving their object, and in wrongly reacting to it. But the emotional response itself, even if later contradicted, represents a firm and confident judgment.

And the same goes for humility. Humility is not an expression of low self-esteem, self- denunciation, ill-confidence, incertitude, indecision, or vacillation. Indeed, it is not a form of self-doubting at all. To candidly own up to one's limitations or failures is not to be *suspicious* of one's capabilities, or wary of one's powers, but to confidently deem them to be lacking. It is a form of self-critique, in which one frankly take the measure of oneself against norms and standards to which one holds. But, as noted, unlike any other form of self-criticism, humility seldomly entails

---

[9] In Brandom's more recent casting of his position in Hegelian terms, the idea of mutual scorekeeping in sharing our reasons with others central to his (1994, 141–143 and *passim*)—is replaced by a more robust notion of "mutual recognition', namely, our dependency on others to hold us to the responsibilities we shoulder, and grant us the authority to do so, and vice versa. For this later phase in his thinking, see Brandom (2009, 68–108), and in its most developed form in Part Two of Brandon (2019) entitled: "Normative Pragmatics: Recognition and the Expressive Metaphysics of Agency".

5.3 Humility's Dialectic and the Split Self

self-rebuke.[10] Humility is bred, we might say, by taking a proud and confident stand against oneself. This is not a contradiction in terms, of course, but it does represent a dispositional dialectic: the more confident the judgment, the more definite the humility it yields.

What enables this uniquely human two-sided disposition owes to the nature of human reflexivity and normative self-assessment, acutely described as a form of self-alienation by Frankfurt, noted above in connection with secondary shame.[11] We are not merely conscious of our desires, beliefs, strengths, and limitations, but hold them in constant critical review. By means of our unique ability to form second-order volitions, in addition to our first-order desires and capacities, we are able to conduct rational self-corrective processes of self-review and self-identification; to identify our limitations and identify *with* the desires and beliefs that we want, or would have wanted to have, and alienate ourselves from those we do not, denying them "any entitlement to supply us with motives or with reasons" (Frankfurt 2004, 4). What lends the seat of our second order volitions, call it our I-part, its special judicial authority is that it is constituted not by what we earnestly want, but by what we earnestly *want to want*, and what we want to want pertains to what we most dearly care about. Our I-part is hence the seat of our norms and standards, the part of us with which, and by which we wholeheartedly identify; by which we determine who we are and who we aspire to be.

Different people harbor different first-order desires, impulses, beliefs, strengths and weaknesses, and with them equally diverse second-order standards and norms—all products of their specific and radically diverse biographies and circumstances. They hold themselves and others accountable to their different norms, measure them according to their different standards and as a result, assess their own strengths and limitations as differently as to whom they aspire to be. Yet different as they are, *human beings nonetheless have in common one fundamental, all-pervasive, severe, universally shared, and exclusively human limitation*, for which to appreciate we need to take a closer look at the role of normativity in both rationality and humility.

To repeat, to act rationally is to act to rectify what one deems to be sufficiently wrong, wanting, or lacking within the purview of one's responsibility to justify intervention with a view to putting it right. To feel humility is to own up to what one perceives one lacks in order to take such action.[12] The fact that all human communities, past and present, universally employ the same vocabulary of thin critically

---

[10] Except incidentally, as when we blame ourselves for the career choices, for example, that rendered us unqualified to do what needed to be done, or when, as a result, we resolve to improve on the weaknesses and limitations to which we owned up. Yet even in the latter case, unlike shame, humor, or guilt, humility is not *directed* at self-improvement. The critical argument employs norms, yet not for the sake of normative indictment. Humility yields an account of what we *are* capable, not of what we *should* be capable, as in other forms of self-criticism.

[11] See n.22 above and accompanying text.

[12] Even if what we're lacking can be remedied, and we resolve to do so (to get back in shape, to enlist in a first-aid course, never to neglect to bring our phone, etc.), with respect to the task immediately at hand, it must be humbly acknowledged, and until put right, outsourced to others.

evaluative concepts such as good and bad, right and wrong, unimpaired and lacking, becoming and repulsive, can be misleading. They are universally employed, yet their specific content varies as radically as do those who employ them. Such terms acquire their particular meanings for those who employ them by means of their respective cultures' vocabularies of *thick* evaluative concepts such as courageous, modest, outspoken, wary, timid and loud, whose normative weight and precise meaning can vary significantly both within and between different cultures.[13] What one perceives as a severe flaw or weakness, others committed differently might deem to be a God-sent blessing. So much so that, as Benbaji and I have argued in detail elsewhere (Fisch and Benbaji 2011, 31–45)), it is impossible to rank significantly different normative frameworks as better or worse in ways acceptable to both, because the very terms "better" and "worse" do not retain a shared, stable meaning across such normative divides.

Rationality, like the humility it requires, is universal: a reasoned willingness to attend to the failings and shortcomings one encounters, to the candidly assessed best of one's ability. Yet, at the same time, the very terms "failing", "shortcoming" and "best" are place holders for significantly, at times dramatically diverse, normative commitments that render both rationality and humility thoroughly framework-dependent. Put differently, our ability to act for reasons, and in doing so to own up to our limitations are human universals, but the reasons we act *for*, and what we perceive as limitations and failings, pertain, not to what we share, but to the broad and ever-shifting diversity of the homegrown norms and ideals that set us markedly apart.

As a result our very notion of rationality is greatly expanded. We hold ourselves accountable to the norms and standards to which we hold, as we hold others to theirs. We expect people to live up to what they are committed to, and criticize them when they do not; calling ourselves and others to task for acting without due reason, or for failing to act as and when we should. We likewise criticize ourselves and others for failing to duly acknowledge our limitations, as well as for underrating our abilities. Prudent humility is a delicate line to toe. All of this, however, pertains to what we might call "first-order normativity," namely, rationality's demand that we prudently evaluate our world and ourselves, and act, and refrain from acting in accord with the standards of propriety to which we are committed.

But in view of the broad diversity of human normative options, rationality demands more. We feel obliged to hold others accountable, and they do us, not only for living up to the norms to which we happen to be committed, but for living up to norms *worthy of living up to*! We regularly criticize religious people for not fully abiding by their religious standards, for failing to attend mass regularly, for instance, or to keep strictly kosher. Conservatives criticize liberals for not acting as liberally

---

[13] For the vast literature on the thick-thin distinction see Pekka Väyrynen's Stanford Encyclopedia of Philosophy entry on "Thick Ethical Concepts", https://plato.stanford.edu/entries/thick-ethical-concepts/ substantively revised February, 2021. For studies of the broader significance and consequences of the distinction, see Walzer's classic (2019) as well as Fisch and Benbaji (2011) especially Part 1.

5.3 Humility's Dialectic and the Split Self

as they preach, and vice versa. But the secular criticize the religious just as regularly for being religious, rather than for not being religious enough, just as liberals most often criticize conservatives for their conservatism, not for not living up to their conservative ideals! And it is here, in aspiring, not merely to holding ourselves to our normative commitments, but to holding to them *rationally*, that a major problem asserts itself, and a fundamental form of humility is rendered a universal must.

To see how let us take a closer look at criticism. To criticize requires framing an argument that resembles an existence proof; one that purports to prove to those criticized that something for which they are responsible is sufficiently amiss to require their attention. For an argument to validly entail that a state of affairs S is seriously amiss, it is necessary that it's premises include (a) assertion(s) P that jointly imply the existence of S, and (b) the assertion of a standard or a norm N of which S is in serious violation. And for it to validly prove so *for those it addresses*, it is necessary that *they* consider P to be true and are committed to N. Put slightly differently, prudent criticism is an addressed speech act in the form of an argument, which to achieve its transformative objective, those it criticizes must endorse as *self-criticism*—if they do not, it will have achieved nothing. To find its mark, prudent criticism must, therefore, be leveled from the perspective of those it criticizes, emulating, as best it can, *their* world-view and values, mounting its case on premises that *they* hold true, and in ways that *they* deem to be valid.[14] More importantly for our present concerns is how self-criticism thus emerges not as a tiny reflexive subset of a much broader category of critical exchange, but as criticism's, and with it as rationality's very objective and quintessential form.

Standing against ourselves in self-critique is a uniquely human achievement made possible by the split nature of the human self. Stepping back from our impulses, desires, tendencies and unconsidered doings, our I-part, the seat of our normative commitments, is able to hold our empirical self in self-critical review, passing judgment on it when it falls short of them, and prompting it to act where we deem self-improvement to be an option. We are also able to self-reflect on the norms our I-part embodies, allowing us to better acquaint ourselves with our commitments, render them explicit, and even troubleshoot them for coherence, clarity and consistency.[15] We hold to norms of varied weight and import, and often dismiss lower-level commitments in the light of those we deem to be more binding, as when we find our department's regulations to be at odds with our liberal or religious

---

[14] To win the trust of those it criticizes, criticism must always be leveled with intimate authenticity from within *their* normative perspectives. Such a thought, I believe, motivates the great emphasis laid by Walzer (1987) on the *connectedness* of effective social criticism.

[15] This is the extent to which both Brandom and McDowell are able to envisage discharging our "critical responsibilities", to use the former's term, toward the entire body of our commitments. Brandom sees it as a responsibility "to weed out materially incompatible commitments ... [by] rejecting candidate judgments that are incompatible with what one is already committed to and responsible for, or relinquishing the offending prior commitments" Brandom (2009, 36). McDowell claims similarly, if more metaphorically, that "the appropriate image" for how we "reflect about and criticize the standards by which [we take ourselves] to be governed" is "Neurath's, in which a sailor overhauls his ship while it is afloat" McDowell (1994, 81).

values. But what is revealed on such occasions is that we were *mistaken*, that we were never truly committed to the lower level norm to begin with. Normative purging in the light of higher-level commitments is how we find out to which norms and standards we are genuinely committed, not whether they *merit* commitment.

And this is where the problem lies. What such critical normative housekeeping can never do in principle, and this is the important point, is to hold the norms to which we are genuinely committed in *normative* check, as they do us. For the simple reason that it is by means of those very norms that we pass such normative judgment! It follows, that as much as we would like to consider our epistemic, moral, political, ethical and religious commitments as having passed critical normative muster, and, subsequently, to have been *rationally* endorsed and committed to by us, there seems to be no non-circular way of doing so. But if we are unable in principle to normatively criticize our norms, we can have no rational reason for holding or for replacing them, and we can, therefore, not be held accountable for them any more than for our physical and psychic makeup!

Yet that seems absurd! To think that real normative commitments are in principle immune to the normative scrutiny of those committed to them; that we can be held no more accountable for our liberal, Darwinian, or religious convictions than for our accents or the color of our skin, seems no less than outrageous!

Casting all of this in emotional terms allows us to better appreciate the problem and to see the beginnings of a possible way out. As noted previously, to criticize another person, or a normative framework that is not one's own, is to adopt a confident, proud stance toward them. Criticism cannot be hypothetical. It aspires to prove the existence of a problem and to hold those criticized responsible for attending to it. To prudently endorse or solicit the criticism of others is, by contrast, to adopt the opposite stance, that of humility. Self-criticism, can, therefore, be tricky. As we have seen, when we call ourselves to task for not living up to the standards we hold to, we act divided, with our I-parts, our normative selves, speaking in the first person, passing confident normative judgment on our empirical selves for not paying sufficient attention, or giving in to weakness or impulse, and our empirical selves humbly accepting its verdict.[16]

But we are privy to no such self-divide capable of facilitating self-critique of our *normative* selves. There is no place for us to stand from which our I-part can act as both proud, confident critic and humbly criticized at one and the same time. This emotional ambivalence, the incoherent close-circuiting of pride and humility involved in genuine normative self-criticism, renders it a real impossibility that can

---

[16] The point is made forcefully by Frankfurt's (1971, §II) well-known distinction between the willing and unwilling addict.

Interestingly, as Rosen-Zvi (2011) shows, the rabbinic literature of late antiquity locates the source of evil, not in one's blind, animalistic impulses and desires, but as mediated by an internal alter-ego-like persona, who, intimately acquainted with both one's knowledge of the ritual law and one's deepest desires, argues and reasons on their behalf to insistently undermine one's commitments.

only be overcome by outsourcing its critical component and assigning it to others.[17] This, I believe, is the unwitting, intuitional import of Sellars and Brandom's insistence on viewing participation in the game of reasons as rationality's ultimate manifestation. But we need to tread carefully.

5.4 The Inimitable Value of Otherness

In one sense Brandom and Sellars's claim seems clear enough. We are often motivated to reveal to others our reasons for acting after the event for apologetic reasons. I doubt, though, that Brandom or Sellars would have considered deeming joining in the game of reasons defensively for this kind of reason as the epitome of rationality. Indeed, apologetics might explain a person's willingness to reveal his reasons for acting in the company of others, but not his interest in theirs. Given their insistence on viewing rational action as action taken for a reason, and of the major role played by self-criticism in such reasoning, it makes sense, as indicated previously, to attribute engaging in giving and asking for reasons to a desire, even after the event, to learn from what fellow agents might make of our reasoning and to offer them our opinion of theirs.[18] But, again, to be considered the very epitome of rationality, this cannot be a matter of idle curiosity, or mere fascination with how other people think.

I noted above[19] that in his more recent work Brandom ceases to view our interaction with others regarding our reasoning as merely inquisitive. To act for a reason is at once to take responsibility for judging a situation, and to claim the authority to intervene or demand that others do so. However, he now argues (with explicit reference to Hegel and echoing Wittgenstein's private language argument) that while it is exclusively up to us to *assume* responsibility for judging and to *claim* the authority to act or to demand that others do so, only others can substantiate such intentions by making them normatively binding on us in *holding* us responsible and *granting* us the *authority* we claim. The space of reasons, one might say, is thus rendered home to two distinct discursive realms: on the one hand, an inherently internal, intra-subjective realm in which one finds reason to act and undertakes to act accordingly, and, on the other, an inherently external, inter-subjective realm of reciprocal *recognition*, in which we recognize one another's responsibility and authority to do so (Brandom 2009, 79–80). Yet, although a step forward, in that he now describes us as engaging others not merely to exchange information about our reasoning, but

---

[17] Alasdair MacIntyre (1988, ch.18), Taylor (1989, 63–75) and later Jaeggi (2018, ch.8) attempt to solve the problem of creating critical distance from our deepest convictions by viewing them genealogically as the products of a dynamic historical process, from which one can create critical distance. However, taking normative stock of former versions of our norms is categorically different from creating such distance from those to which we are now committed, and with which we perform such critical assessments.

[18] On reason and reasoning see Raz (2011, 87–90).

[19] See above §5.3, n.9 and accompanying text.

54   5 The Humble Self

for their necessary acknowledgement, a major component remains disturbingly lacking from Brandom's account.

Not unlike our notion of the I-part, Brandom has also come to identify the self or the subject as the totality of her commitments, whom he charges, among other things, with the *critical* responsibility for locating and resolving any inconsistencies and incoherence within it and integrating new commitments among the old. Following Kant he terms the self-defining integrated body of a person's commitments a "synthetic unity of apperception" (2009, 36–40). And the same applies, he submits, to determining the public, shared body of inferentially related conceptual contents availed to the community by processes of reciprocal recognition among its members. Here too, as the image of the common law judge he borrows from Hegel clearly implies, critical responsibility for rendering it a consistent unified whole, falls exclusively to the individual "judge", who, in making her decisions, endorses certain prior rulings as binding precedents while refusing such status to others (2009, 84–88).

The role of criticism is thus confined in Brandom's account to trouble-shooting one's commitments for inconsistencies and unclarity, and trawling the tradition for commitments supportive of one's own. Hence, what goes wholly missing from his complex picture of rational agency and its social and historical settings, is *exposure to the critique of others*, past or present, to which he assigns no role at all in the discharge of a person's critical responsibilities. Like common-law judges sifting through past rulings, Brandomian agents engage one another to enjoy the support of those with whom they agree, and the recognition of those who hold them responsible, to the dismissal of those who do not. He is well aware that experts are in possession of information concerning concepts that other people lack, and that we consult them both to learn more and to correct our misconceptions. But their criticism is limited to knowing that, and knowing how, and does not resemble the kind of normative critique leveled across normative divides that we are concerned with here, for which his account makes no room.[20]

However, the fact that reciprocal recognition came to replace the game of giving asking for reasons in Brandom's system, doesn't mean that it has to. Discussing our reasons with others, deliberating with them, taking their opinions to heart and acquainting ourselves with how people committed differently from us think, are all of intrinsic value over and above the acknowledgment we grant and receive in reciprocal recognition of their normative attitudes and actions and theirs of ours. The development of Brandom's thinking might seem to imply that the idea of viewing the game of reasons as the hallmark of rationality must give way to, and be replaced by that of reciprocal recognition. It indeed seems to do so in Brandom's thinking, but is nowhere explained. Which is surprising since the two modes of mutual interaction, are by no means incompatible.

---

[20] See his distinction between wanting to be a formidable chess player, as opposed to being recognized as one, and the scientific example of recognizing a copper coin, and knowing its exact melting temperature in Brandom (2009, 70–74).

5.4 The Inimitable Value of Otherness

One way to see why is to realize that recognition is indifferent to agreement. On the contrary. Nothing better acknowledges another person's responsibility and claim to authority in acting than taking a firm stand *against* her reasoning and actions. Recognizing a person's agency and approving her reasoning and actions are two quite different things. Being prompted to articulate our reasons for acting, and prompting others to disclose theirs are not requests for recognition, but are aimed at airing and exploring our differences. The game of reasons, I insist, supervenes on self-doubt, criticism and justification, and is played primarily for approval, not merely for recognition.

Like the reflexive emotions examined here, participation in the game of reasons is an exclusively human undertaking. If the ability to identify and respond to reasons goes to the heart or the essence of human rationality, as Raz (2011) has it, then the second-order activity of articulating and deliberating what we identify as reasons and how we respond to them constitutes a reflective, and therefore elevated level of rational endeavor. But, again, only if it is genuinely deliberative, neither defensive nor idle. In other words, only if it is truly self-directed. The question is what added value can there be in self-deliberating aloud in the company of others? The obvious answer lies in the kind of outsourcing for which humility calls.

But how? We have seen that as much as we would like it is impossible for us to create critical distance from our own heartfelt norms. To normatively criticize a norm we are committed to is to deem it in some sense normatively wrong or inappropriate. But by what standard of wrongness can we judge our very standards of wrongness and impropriety to be wrong or inappropriate? Adopting such a stand against ourselves, as we have seen, is impossible. Others can criticize our norms, of course. We have no problem disapproving of another person's convictions and declaring them wrong from the point of view of our own. It is tempting, therefore, to locate human rationality at its best in being aware of our inability to hold our own norms in normative check, and humbly enlisting others to do so for us. We enlist others regularly whenever we doubt our own judgment, consider ourselves unqualified for the task at hand, too close to be objective, too involved, lack the necessary know-how, or be otherwise biased, and ask for their opinion. And this would seem to be the reason for Sellars and the early Brandom's contention that engaging in the reasons game be considered the highest form of rationality.

All this would have made perfect sense if the aim of exposing our reasons to others was to receive an *objective* opinion regarding our motives and actions. But that is not at all the case. The very aim of prudently criticizing someone else, as we have seen, is not to try to be objective at all, but to level one's critical argument as best one can from the perspective of the person one is criticizing; to explain to her not why we think differently, as most people do, but to prove to her that given *her* commitments and circumstances, we believe that *she* should have reasoned and acted differently, emulating as best as possible *her* point of view! And here it would seem that prudent external normative critique necessarily shares the exact same glass ceiling that marks the upper possible limit of normative self-critique. For, if to be effective, criticizing other people's norms must roundly model itself on effective normative self-criticism on *their* part, then it can never be effective for the simple reason that there is no such thing as effective self-critique of anybody's own norms! As much as we would like to acknowledge our limitations by humbly outsourcing the normative critique of our commitments to others, no one, it would seem, can, in principle, do so in our stead!

And yet, we have all experienced how in friendly conversation with people committed differently, we are able to reflect more critically on those of our norms they question. How is that possible? Can it be more than an illusionary internalizing of *their* critical distance. Can people committed differently prudently doing their best to argue as we would, nonetheless present us with something we are unable to present ourselves? When it comes to criticism, can there be additional value to an honest imitation over the original? Curious as it may sound, I believe the answer is "yes". Paradoxically, the reason that exposure to external criticism can help us create normative critical distance from our own convictions is that, try as they may, external normative critics cannot but be *not completely* truthful (in one of two senses of the necessity implied). Let me explain.

For their critical arguments against a person's norms to be effective, external critics must argue from premises they believe he can hold true. The problem, as we've seen, is that unless the framework he is committed to is hopelessly incoherent, such premises are never forthcoming. For to argue from *his* point of view that norms to which *he* is committed are normatively wanting, requires premising a commitment of *his own* from which this follows—one to which he can never coherently hold. And even if it were possible to frame such an argument in a way that the person it criticizes somehow deems valid, and from premises he somehow holds true, it would still fail to convince him because he would still consider its conclusion utterly unacceptable.

The idea of declaring a norm to which we are genuinely committed normatively deficient, is intolerable, and seemingly valid arguments from seemingly impeccable premises to such preposterous conclusions are easily set aside. We call them paradoxes: disturbing tantalizing, seemingly irrefutable arguments that we know *have to* be wrong, although we are currently unable to explain their wrongness. Although irrefutable in their time, Zeno's paradoxes, for instance, convinced very few that change was impossible, and that the very notion of velocity (change of location in time) was incoherent. His arguments were simply set aside as bafflingly amusing for over two millennia until new mathematical advances enabled their reasoned rejection. Logic alone is powerless to deracinate a heartfelt norm.

Nonetheless, to be effective and find their mark critical arguments must be leveled on the basis of premises that those they criticize hold true. Yet at the same time, there is never available a set of premises a person is liable to consider true, that can be shown, convincingly *for him*, to entail a denunciation of his very norms, and even if there was, the argument would never convince him. How, then, can external normative criticism ever have its desired effect?

I believe that to some extent prudent critics know, or at least sense that it is indeed impossible to level their arguments from squarely *within* the worldview of those they criticize. But they also know, or at least sense that in order to make its mark their criticism must be leveled *as close as possible* from premises whom those

5.4 The Inimitable Value of Otherness

they criticize will recognize as their own. Therefore, they frame their criticism to an extent *untruthfully*, arguing from a perspective close to that of their addressees, yet sufficiently different from it to be able to at least mount a valid argument. Arguing from the left, critics surreptitiously attribute certain liberal norms to those they criticize so as to make their case, while those arguing from the right, tend to smuggle in just enough conservative value to make their arguments stick. We have all experienced this kind of exchange.

Most of the time, however, people do so unthinkingly, with no intention of being untruthful. Whether we like it or not our normative assessments of others—the expectations we frame, the disappointment and frustration we register in the light of their reasoning and conduct—emphatic and open-minded as they may aspire to be, are ultimately conditioned by our own normative outlooks rather than by theirs. When we are disturbed by someone's conduct to the point of protesting we are measuring it by a normative yardstick *we* strongly feel *should* be hers. We are hence liable to accuse her of betraying norms that are in fact not her own. Our moral outrage owes to the fact that she fails to live up to the person *we* strongly believe that she believes she should be. In other words, when openly and prudently criticizing elements of another person's wholeheartedly held normative framework to her face, we will inevitably be arguing against them from a picture of her I-part which is most likely to be importantly different from the real thing, as it were, motivated by the deep conviction that it *should* be true.

Either way, when our norms are prudently criticized by others we are most liable to be confronted by a part-portrayal of our normative framework, which, though largely true to it, differs noticeably from our own self-image.[21]

Since leveled against heartfelt norms, we will inevitably dismiss the argument's conclusion. And yet the picture of our normative identity conveyed by its premises, may linger on and register uncoupled from the argument itself. Such deontic portrayals need not be deemed *true* for them to resonate and disturb. It is enough that we consider them *sincere*; to realize that trusted others see us differently from how we see ourselves. Since the two pictures—our own normative self-portrayal, and that conveyed by our critic—will diverge precisely with regard to the very norms she questions. The two portrayals' incongruity, not unlike the case of a disturbing *playback device*, may well have the effect of rendering us ambivalent toward those norms. And norms to which we become ambivalent lose their I-part status as firm commitments, and will inevitably be subjected to the normative critical self-scrutiny

---

[21] Despite the objectivist turn of phrase of the previous paragraph, the discrepancy on which the dynamic I'm describing rides has nothing to do with the person criticized's *real* I-part, but with what she takes it to be. Figuring out who we are, what is truly important to us and to what we are genuinely committed is a never-ending and constantly shifting project of self-learning, dotted by moments of self-revelation as we find ourselves reacting to new circumstances and challenges, and even to therapy. The title of the second of Frankfurt's Tanner Lectures—"Getting it Right"—can be misleading. We can never know for certain that we've gotten ourselves right. Doing so, as Frankfurt more than implies at the very end of the book (Frankfurt 2006, 278, n.1), resembles the confidence we develop toward what Descartes dubbed "clear and distinct", if forever unprovable ideas. For a more recent study along these lines see Phillips (2024)

of our surviving commitments. This, I believe, is how exposure to trusted normative criticism can at times *induce* a level of inner-discordance and self-alienation sufficient for us to truly change our minds, despite the fact that such criticism can never convince.

The image of a playback device, of hearing a recording or seeing a video of ourselves addressing an audience, for example, is worth dwelling upon. Although the images of us they convey often diverges, even jars with our own self-image, we clearly recognize ourselves in them. And it is by virtue of this coupling of familiarity and incongruity that they can have the critical, even transformative effect so many of us have experienced. They achieve it not by *convincing* us that we look, move, or sound differently than we think we do, but by destabilizing our confidence in how we imagine ourselves. It is the very jarring closeness of the two that renders us ambivalent. Yet it is not because we have come to trust our eyes and ears more than our in-built sense of how we seem and sound. We can never see or hear ourselves directly as we do others. The recording device mediates their external viewpoint for us, but we do not experience its uptake as vested with the same adjudicating objectifying authority as we deem that of other experiential aids and instruments. Caught in the cross lights of the view from within and the device's mediated view from without, we dither undecided, rendered uncertain of our very sense of self.

Most importantly, the vantage point afforded to us by the recording device is one we are incapable in principle of occupying unassisted by it. And yet it is a vantage point without which we are incapable of creating critical distance from whom we think we are. Exposure to such devices, as we can all attest, can be a humbling experience, but acknowledging their indispensability to our ability to hold our self-image in self-critical review and knowingly subjecting ourselves to such an experience, is an *act* of true humility.

In terms of the demands of rationality, there is of course no comparison between the requirement to hold our normative commitments in normative check, and to gain a self-critical grip on how we believe we look or sound. Creating critical distance from the norms to which we are wholeheartedly committed is what can lend them *rational* normative force for us—a question quite different from the *authority* to commit ourselves to them vouched for by the recognition of others of which Hegel and Brandom make so much. Norms acquire their hold on us by habit, rote, acculturation, and indoctrination. But, as noted, for our commitment to them to be deemed rational, they must pass normative critical muster, and for this, exposure to external normative critique is mandatory.

Such exposure can be accidental or deliberate; encountered by chance, or sought for rationally. To do so rationally is to do so for a reason bred of being knowingly aware (a) of our inability ever to create such distance by talking to ourselves or to like-minded community members, and (b) of how exposure to the echo-chamber of critics committed differently is the only way open to us to do so. It is in this sense, I submit, that engaging true others in the game of giving and asking for reasons *for that reason* can be genuinely considered rationality's high point, as Sellars and Brandom insist it is without ever explaining why.

The point is quite general and applies equally to any human agent regardless of the particular norms to which he or she are committed. The unbreachable constraints normative commitments place on the rationality of those whose norms they are is a human universal, just as is the fact that they can only be rationally breached when the bearers of those commitments become duly ambivalated toward them by exposure to external normative critique. And because it is only by humbly *owning up* to the normative limits of our ability to self-critique and acting upon them by actively seeking the normative critique of others that we can live up to our full rational capacity, I deem engaging in the game of reasons for this reason to be, not only the utmost form of rationality, but also the utmost form of humility.

There are many ways to be rendered normatively ambivalent, some surreptitious, as when we awaken unexpectedly to being of two minds toward something we had cherished or abhorred, others more manifest, as when ambivalated by a significant change of events or circumstance. But in all such cases ambivalence is something that happens to happen to us involuntarily, not something we are able to actively pursue. By contrast, the only potentially ambivalating set of circumstances we can contrive knowingly, and hence rationally to experience is exposure to normative criticism leveled at us by meaningful others. It is also the only set of potentially ambivalating circumstances we can be motivated to pursue by force of a reflexive emotional response: humility; an honest owning up to our inability, in principle, to hold the norms we're committed to in normative check, and outsourcing it to others. The next chapter explores an additional class of reflexive emotions, which though capable of prompting normative ambivalence, like all emotions, can hardly be rationally affected.

Bibliography

Brandom RB (1994) Making it explicit: reasoning, representing and discursive commitment. Harvard University Press, Cambridge, MA

Brandom RB (2002) Tales of the mighty dead: historical essays in the metaphysics of intentionality. Harvard University Press, Cambridge, MA

Brandom RB (2009) Reason in philosophy: animating ideas. Harvard University Press, Cambridge, MA

Brandon RB (2019) A spirit of trust: a reading of Hegel's *Phenomenology*. Harvard University Press, Cambridge, MA

Fisch M (2025) Dialogues of reason: science, politics, religion. Echter Verlag Wuerzburg

Fisch M, Benbaji Y (2011) The view from within: normativity and the limits of self-criticism. University of Notre Dame Press, South Bend

Frankfurt HG (1971) Freedom of will and the concept of a person. J Philos 67(1):5–20

Frankfurt HG (2004) The reasons of love. Princeton University Press, Princeton

Frankfurt HG (2006) Taking ourselves seriously and getting it right. Stanford University Press, Stanford

Jaeggi R (2018) Critique of forms of life (trans: Cronin C). Harvard University Press, Cambridge MA

Kellenberger J (2010) Humility. Am Philos Q 47(4):321–336

MacIntyre A (1988) Whose justice, which rationality. University of Notre Dame Press, South Bend

McDowell J (1994) Mind and world. Harvard University Press, Cambridge, MA

Murray A (2013) Humility & absolute surrender. CreateSpace, Scotts Valley

Phillips A (2024) On giving up. Penguin Books, London

Raz JI (2011) From normativity to responsibility. Oxford University Press, Oxford

Rosen-Zvi I (2011) Demonic desires: Yetzer Hara and the problem of evil in late antiquity. University of Pennsylvania Press, Philadelphia

Taylor C (1989) Sources of the self: the making of the modern identity. Harvard University Press, Cambridge, MA

Walzer M (1987) Interpretation and social criticism (The Tanner lectures on human values 1985). Harvard University Press, Cambridge, MA

Walzer M (2019) Thick and thin: moral argument at home and abroad, 2nd and revised edn. University of Notre Dame Press, South Bend

Whitcomb D, Batterly H, Baehr J, Howard-Snyder D (2017) Intellectual humility and owning our limitations. Philos Phenomenol Res 94(3):509–539

Chapter 6
Second-Order Emotions

Abstract Against the backdrop of Rahel Jeaggi's critique of Harry Frankfurt's theory of personhood the chapter analyzes the normative import of second-order emotions. The idea is that a disapproving second-order emotional response to a first-order emotional responses that takes us aback, constitutes a moment of normative ambivalence prompted by the unanticipated turn of events that initially gave rise to the first-order response. In view of the crucial role played by normative ambivalation in rational normative self-criticism, to what extent can such moments be sought proactively?

Keywords Second-order emotions · Self-discovery · Normative self-disapproval · Rahel Jaeggi · Alienation · Authenticity · Ambivalence · Richard Rorty

There is a lot more to say about reflexive emotions in general and about each of the many reflexive emotions on which this brief monograph has not been able to touch. From a cognitivist perspective, reflexive, self-directed emotional responses constitute an important, little studied, and humanly unique class of self-evaluation that requires levels of self-awareness to which no other creature or artificial Intelligence is privy. Only humans can be genuinely proud of their achievements, rejoice in them, be wary of their tempers, ashamed of what they do, mourn the loss of their youth, and fear death, which are all emotional deemings of what we find creditable, threatening or lacking in our image of who we are. But second-order emotions, our emotional responses to our emotional responses, form a reflexive class of emotions all to themselves.

© The Author(s), under exclusive license to Springer Nature
Switzerland AG 2025
M. Fisch, *Reflexive Emotions*, SpringerBriefs in Philosophy,
https://doi.org/10.1007/978-3-031-83764-7_6

6.1 Emotions *Versus* Volitions

All emotional responses are judgments that, to some extent, can be reasoned with. But unlike other forms of evaluation, emotion is never a deliberated or considered response. We are often able to control our feelings when deemed necessary—to conceal our fear, contain our grief, hide our amusement. We can also act as if sad, fearful or merry, but when genuine—whether concealed or not—our emotions register verdicts that are passed firmly, spontaneously and involuntarily. We cannot decide or choose to be genuinely sad, anxious, or happy. Emotional responses can be reasoned with, but not undertaken *for* a reason. They express wholly instinctive acts of judging.

Second-order emotions are different from other reflexive emotions, because they react spontaneously to our spontaneous reactions, rather than to our known features, character traits, strengths and weaknesses, considered actions or anticipated reactions. They hence, almost by definition, register surprise.

Anticipatable first-order emotional reactions, even when sudden, will not of themselves trigger a second-order emotional reaction, as when we rejoice over a surprising home-team win, lament the sudden death of a loved one, rage against an unexpected insult, or dread a startling political development. Because anticipated, such expressions of joy, sadness, anger and fear resemble other of our known tendencies and characteristic responses, about which we may have a strong, even emotional opinion, yet response to them will always remain generic. Thus, we might be generally embarrassed by our tendency to go overboard when our team scores and proud of being genuinely saddened by a close friend's misfortune, but we feel joy and pride in such cases even when they're only imagined. In that sense, they are not real second-order emotions, they're more like complex first-order emotional responses, as when one is embarrassingly happy, proudly sad, worryingly indifferent, or jealously in love—cases of unproblematic, non-contradictory mixed feelings, if you wish.

The kind of first-order emotions to which we do react emotionally are those that catch us off guard, and unsuspecting; when not the intensity of what we feel takes us aback, or the unexpectedness of what prompted it, but the very fact that we feel what we feel. We often dismiss such reactions as inconsequential glitches, refusing to allow them to reflect who we really are, as when we chuckle in response to an inappropriate joke or respond impatiently to an anxious student. But when such unanticipated responses strike us, as they often do, as authentically self-expressive, the second-order emotional reaction to which they give rise will normally express more than an evaluation. Second-order emotions of this kind represent moments of self-discovery and self-learning that can be significant.

A spontaneous emotional reaction will give rise to a second-order spontaneous emotional reaction only when the former is both unforeseen, yet deemed authentic, in which case, the second-order emotion it elicits will register the pleasure or displeasure, pride or shame, fear or relief, grief or joy we instinctively feel toward the formerly unbeknownst side of us of which we have abruptly been made aware. But

6.1 Emotions *Versus* Volitions

of what exactly have we become aware in such cases? To repeat, first-order emotional responses are judgments that deem objects and events we care about to be amusing or saddening, pleasing or worrying, etc. They impart value for us upon the welcomed presence or preferred absence of the objects and events they respond to. Emotional responses represent, therefore, inherently *normative* judgments. The "for us"—or as Nussbaum prefers, the eudaimonistic—element in each emotional response transforms the judgment it passes from a merely factual assertion to a personal normative appraisal. When we experience fear, sadness, or joy, we are not merely noting the presence or occurrence of something fearful, joyful, or sad to some, most, or all, but deeming the presence or occurrence of something as fearful or sad to *me*, and hence unwelcome, or as pleasing or joyous, and hence more than welcome to me. These are evaluations that we make, or express emotionally on the basis of the values, norms and standards to which we are personally committed. It follows that when we experience a second-order emotion we are passing normative judgment on a normative judgment of our own; deeming it to be, not normatively valid or mistaken, but normatively *approved* or *condemned*.

In other words, when we're saddened by secretly rejoicing in a rival's failure, disgusted by dreading to stand up to a superior, or proud of reacting with compassion toward a stranger in need, we'll be normatively affirming or condemning the value judgments expressed by the first-order emotion we're reacting to—not to their success, or to the accuracy of their factual basis, but to the *appropriateness* of the norm or standard deployed by them. Second-order emotions thus have much in common with Frankfurtian second-order volitions. Second-order emotional reactions stand to the first-order emotional reactions they react to, just as second-order volitions stand to the first-order volitions they approve or condemn. Second-order emotions determine which first-order emotions we want to feel, and which we prefer not to have felt, just as second-order volitions determine which first-order desires we want to have and be effective and which we'd prefer not to. In thus doing, our second-order emotions hold our first-order emotional reactions in normative check, as do our second-order volitions with respect to our first-order desires.

But there is a major difference. First-order desires express brute inclinations, attractions, and repulsions, and of themselves harbor no normative content. They do not constitute judgments, but for cognitivists like the present author, first-order emotions do. They are different from first-order volitions in manifesting normative preference which is imparted on their objects by virtue of their eudaimonistic nature.[1]

---

[1] Which also drives a wedge, unacknowledged by Nussbaum, between human and animal emotion. Human emotions adopt a critical stance toward what gives rise to them—a worrying prospect, something fearful, a joyous event, an endearing person—deeming them to be problematic, threatening, lacking, worthy, or welcome for the person in question—all normative categories relating to his or her personal commitments. Although such judgments are passed unthinkingly, they can be made explicit in conversation, which can never be said about animal emotion. Animals feel and in their actions express grief, fright, and joy, but cannot be said to be passing normative judgment in doing so any more than they can be said to harbor normative commitments. In this sense, despite

Our I-Part, the sum of our second-order volitions, constitutes the seat of the binding commitments to which we aspire and by which we self-govern, among other things, by holding our first-order impulses and desires in normative check. But in passing normative judgment on our first-order emotions, our second-order emotions seem to be able to do the impossible on our behalf: to normatively criticize our own norms. Because all emotions are norm-laden, to coin a term, second-order emotions pass normative judgment on the very normative basis of the first order emotions to which they react. But the norms they approve or condemn are ours!

Normative self-approval is not problematic, except for being uninterestingly circular.[2] It is when a second-order emotion registers normative self-*dis*approval that it expresses a form of normative self-critique I have argued is impossible, as when we're saddened by reacting joyously, fearful of our dread, ashamed of our amusement.

6.2 Judging *Versus* Arguing

But we need to tread a little more carefully. The first thing to note is that what I argued was impossible is for a person to frame an *argument* normatively self-critical of her own norms. It is impossible because for such an argument to validly conclude *for her* that standards of rightness to which she is committed are wrong, it must premise a standard of wrongness to which she is equally committed normatively condemning it, which by definition is never forthcoming unless her normative framework is hopelessly incoherent. But then emotions, are *not* arguments.

Emotions are evaluative judgments, often disapproving, but they are not *reasoned* evaluative judgments. They state our preferences as a matter of normatively laden fact, but do not argue for them. Frankfurt (2004) speaks of "reasons of love", but only in the sense of love motivating what we do and think, not of our reasons *for* loving. In a manner of speaking, emotions function as reasons for acting, for hiding

---

bodily resemblance, animal emotion is more akin to first-order non-cognitive human desire than to cognitive human emotion.

[2] Uninterestingly circular only in the sense that, by virtue of our very commitment to them, norms we are committed to do not require further normative approval. Still, approving second-order emotions can be highly, and untrivially informative in other ways. Sometimes it's not its normative basis *per se*, but the intensity or depth of the first-order emotion that takes us aback and is approved. At any point in time we know ourselves only to a certain degree, we have witnessed ourselves reacting, are aware of how we think, and how we imagine ourselves reacting in circumstances we've never experienced. But before we actually go to war, experience true love, are separated from someone close, win the lottery, or are faced with a heart wrenching dilemma, we can never be sure how we will end up reacting, however much we have imagined, desired, or dreaded being in such circumstances. These can be trying moments in which we are made aware of how different we may turn out to be from whom we imagined we are. When we do better than we thought we could, as when finding ourselves genuinely feeling for someone we weren't sure we could, or less fearful in situations we dreaded, our second-order approving emotion does more than affirm the norm at play, at times it affirms our capacity to live up to it beyond our wildest expectations.

6.2 Judging *Versus* Arguing

from what we fear, for devoting ourselves to whom we love, for emulating whom we admire, but only in a manner of speaking. Reasons, at least when talked of in Brandomian terms, stand in *inferential* relations to the beliefs and actions whose reasons they are. The space of reasons is a space of (material) entailment. It is logical. Our commitments *entitle* us to what they entail by virtue of entailing it.[3] Emotions, by contrast, motivate us to take action, but do not *entitle* us to take it. Fearing something might justify running from it, but it does not *authorize* us to do so.

Emotions harbor motive force but have no logical force or authority. They do not stand in strict inferential relations to what prompts them or to the reactions to which they give rise. It is, therefore, highly doubtful that despite their cognitive nature, normative content, and explanatory power, emotional responses can at all be granted entry into the space of reasons. Yet because of their cognitive nature and normative content, it seems equally absurd to confine them merely to the space of causes. One cannot reason with brute causal force!

Emotions thus seem to form a class of their own, located somewhere between bona fide mindful purpose and mindless compulsion: falling short on the one hand, of constituting full-fledged reasons, yet far transcending mere impulse, certainly from a cognitivist perspective; constituting spontaneous, yet at the same time intentional judgments. In view of the central role they play in all manner of human consideration, deliberation and decision making, the question of locating the emotions between the pushes and pulls of human mindedness cannot be brushed aside by cognitivists. It certainly seriously challenges the seemingly firm dichotomy between the space of reasons and that of brute cause implied by Sellars and his followers, primarily Brandom and McDowell—a question I hope to take up elsewhere.[4]

In the present context, I am less concerned with the role played by emotions in reasoning than in the nature and significance of their capacity for norm-laden self-appraisal, especially when negative. And here, with respect to second-order emotions, a second distinction is in order.

Some emotions represent more permanent, ongoing states of mind like the love, respect, hate, or fear we feel toward the people, ideas, institutions, and states of affairs that form part of our ongoing lives. Other emotional responses represent more spur-of-the-moment, ad hoc responses to new experiences and encounters. Normatively speaking, emotional states of the first kind express commitments of which we are well aware. They teach us little new, except perhaps when they express themselves with unexpected intensity or lack of it, and, therefore, as remarked above, when they hold to a familiar and normal keel, they seldom give rise to

---

[3] Brandom (2000, chs.1&2).

[4] In his seminal "Self-Interpreting Animals", Taylor (1985, ch.2) forcefully describes our self-referring emotions to be no less than "our mode of access to ...what it is to be human. ...Our self-referring feelings ...open us on to what it is to be human; for we have no dispassionate awareness of the human good; and the quality of our awareness of the good is a function of the alignment of our feelings" (62–63).

second-order emotional reactions.[5] As noted further, second-order emotional reactions are largely reactions to first-order emotions that catch us off guard, and inasmuch as they register a negative response, such as fear, shame, sorrow, or guilt, they represent authentic (because spontaneous) norm-based condemnations of first-order norm-based emotional reactions—not critical arguments, but normative condemnations nonetheless.

6.3 Jaeggi *Versus* Frankfurt

To return for a moment to volitions. Jaeggi (2014, ch.7) criticizes Frankfurt's distinction between first- and second-order volitions, calling to task in particular his claim that it is the latter with which we univocally identify. According to Frankfurt, our second-order volitions are what enable us to alienate ourselves from those of our first-order impulses and desires that they deem to be unwanted. Jaeggi claims, by contrast, that a person can never be sure which of her conflicting volitions is really hers and which are not. The example she gives is that of "the giggling feminist" (100–101), namely, a "self-professed reflective feminist of strong convictions" who catches herself repeatedly "communicating with her lover like a silly, giggling adolescent", which she experiences "as not really part of herself". And yet, she is "internally divided", unable to control herself despite not being able to identify with her "impulse to giggle."

For Frankfurt, it is obvious that the woman's emancipated feminist convictions and unemancipated giggly side, though qualitatively incompatible, are both authentically hers. For him, however, her feminist convictions nonetheless constitute second-order volitions, by means of which she does her best to alienate herself from her impulse to giggle and suppress it as best she can, if not always successfully. Jaeggi disagrees. The only way to resolve such a conflict of desires, she argues, undermining Frankfurt's very distinction between first- and second-order volitions, is to determine "what we *really* want", namely, which of the two "corresponds more to oneself … [which] better represents [her] authentic desires"? When, in other words, "is she really herself", when giggling with her lover, or when reprimanding herself for doing so? One cannot alienate oneself from oneself, she claims (102–103).

What Jaeggi fails to appreciate is the *normative* force of second-order desires—desires about desires; desires expressive, not merely of what we want, but of what we *want to want*. The woman's giggly impulse in her example is not a second-order desire, but a first-order craving that, in light of her strong feminist convictions, she

---

[5] With the exception, of course, of the rare well-known, ongoing emotional states of mind, of which we are perpetually pleased or displeased, fearful, ashamed, or proud, and to which we react emotionally as a matter of course. But as noted previously, when an ongoing emotional state of mind gives rise to an equally ongoing reaction to it, the net result can often be less a case of normative overriding, than of a complex mixed, first-order emotional response, as when one feels embarrassingly happy, or for that matter, a case of emotional ambivalence, that I shall address shortly.

6.3 Jaeggi *Versus* Frankfurt

gives in to. The two desires, both present, both hers, certainly contradict one another, but their relationship is by no means reciprocal or symmetric. In her giggly moments she does not wish she wasn't a feminist. These moments carry no such normative conviction. They represent an authentic first-order craving to act the little girl to be protected and adored by her lover; a craving that resembles hunger rather than judgment.[6] Her equally authentic feminist convictions entail, among other things, a desire to promote desires she has and approves of, to acquire certain desires she does not, and to suppress those she condemns—among them, her giggly, girly impulse. Jaeggi describes the problem of alienation as that of being able to decide which of two qualitatively conflicting desires is really, authentically ours, because in order to alienate oneself from one of them, the other has to be shown to be the more authentic.

But Jaeggi misses Frankfurt's main point. What lends force and authority to our second-order volitions owes not to their relative authenticity, force, or to the extent to which they reflect who we really are. It owes to the extent to which they envisage whom *we want to be.* A powerful second-order volition could well be a newcomer, as when, rocked by a life-changing encounter or experience we resolve to change our ways. Whether it became our will by arousing something deep inside us, or by alerting us to new possibilities we'd never envisaged is wholly aside the point. Following Charles Taylor's observations, second-order volitions can be shallow or deep, weak or strong, and we might add stupid or profound. We all harbor fantasies about who we'd rather be, some silly and childish, some serious, some profound. Some such yearnings pertain to what we want or fail to want. We long to have desires we no longer have, and to rid ourselves of desires that we do. And these can vary significantly in seriousness, strength and depth. Taylor's clever example of the two overweight diners mentioned above makes the point forcefully.[7]

But the depth, strength and seriousness of our second-order volitions are not gauged by Jaeggi's yardstick of authenticity, and certainly not by the relative force of the first-order desires they target. In fact, when speaking of alienation, as does Jaeggi, quite the opposite is true. For Jaeggi, one is whom one is, and can, therefore, only alienate herself from what she isn't, or at least from desires that are only weakly or marginally her own. One does so by means of a conflicting desire that is both stronger and more central to whom she is. One cannot alienate oneself, Jaeggi implies, from what is authentically part of the self one is. By contrast, Frankfurt's picture comprises two selves: one's empirical self, namely, whom one is (to the best of one's knowledge), and one's desired self, namely, the self one does her utmost to make her own. According to Frankfurt, both selves are in one respect, equally really ours. But at a different level, it is the desired self, the seat of our second-order volitions along with the first-order volitions of which they approve, that is more really ours, not by virtue of it being more authentic, but by virtue of our wanting it. For it is our desired, rather than empirical self that speaks for us in the first person, and

---

[6] Unless it is feigned instrumentally for a reason, in which case it would not count as authentic.

[7] See above §3.3.2, n.16 and accompanying text.

governs its empirical counterpart by scrutinizing our first-order desires, instincts, character traits, and impulses, identifying with some, and rejecting, or denying others a part in whom we authentically *desire* to be.[8]

From a Frankfurtian perspective the verb forms of "identity" and "alienation", the twin terms that chart the dynamic borderline between the endorsed and rejected elements of our empirical self, are *transitive* verbs. In Jaeggi's account of alienation they are not. According to Jaeggi, one *finds* (as opposed to makes) a desire or compulsion, such as the giggly impulse of the woman of her example, *to be* alien to oneself, and therefore unworthy of being deemed to be really hers to begin with. On a Frankfurtian showing, one actively *renders* such an unwanted first-order impulse or desire alien to oneself by *refusing* it a place among the effective desires one *wants to have*, whether we end up having it or not.

In fact, an unwanted desire or urge we succeed in repressing to the point of termination, as when successfully kicking a habit such as smoking or losing the taste for sugary foods, the word alienation no longer seems appropriate. Frankfurt's above-mentioned classic distinction between a willing and unwilling addict is a case in point.[9] Both addicts are incapable of resisting the drug. The unwilling addict continues to take it against his will, powerless to oppose his addiction, he views his uncontrollable craving for it as an alien force he is too weak to fight but would have liked to if he only could. He views his craving as an alien force not because he *perceives* it as inauthentic and not really his, but because he genuinely *wills* it not to be his, even if unsuccessfully. The willing addict, by contrast, perceives his craving as authentic and as an integral component of his identity, again because he wills it to be.

What Frankfurt's volitional account of personhood nicely brings to the fore is the essential *agential* nature of the twin intrasubjective acts of self-formation (or as Korsgaard (2009) prefers: self-constitution), namely self-alienation and self-identification. Rather than worry about who we really are by viewing the stock of our desires, tendencies and impulses as on a par, and comparing them for weight, strength or authenticity, Frankfurt conceives us as pressing our second-order volitions into active service in an ongoing effort to fashion ourselves to our liking. And the reason this is possible owes to the inherently *normative* basis of our second-order desires that authorizes them to drive a prescriptive wedge between those of our first-order desires, character traits, impulses, and urges we approve and those we do not, and in doing so, drive and fuel an ongoing dynamic of self-betterment.

---

[8] This is as close as Frankfurt gets to Brandom's employment of Kant's idea of a "synthetic unity of apperception" (Kant 1999, B135), as synonymous to "self or subject" (Brandom (2009, 35–36) noted above §5.4). The main difference between the two notions of self is that Frankfurt grounds it in the will and Brandom in cognition, which enables Frankfurt to distinguish between orders of volition that lend his account of personhood and agency a fundamentally normative structure wholly absent from Kant's First Critique, and Brandom's appropriation of it, as well as from Jaeggi's approach.

[9] See above §3.3.2, n.19, and §5.3, n.16 above.

6.4 The Curious Status of Second-Order Emotions

Back to emotion. Emotional responses, we have noted, can be layered as in Frankfurt's account of volition. Second-order emotions are emotional reactions to first-order emotional responses. They are layered in the sense that they are prompted by categorically different entities. First order emotions respond to entities, persons and states of affairs that move or alarm us, while second-order emotions react to our emotions. In this sense they are as layered as Frankfurtian volitions. But in a different sense they are not. Frankfurtian volitions are not only layered, but form a hierarchy. By virtue of their norm-ladenness, second-order volitions pass final judgment on their normatively neutral first-order counterparts. By contrast, both orders of emotion are equally norm-laden. Second-order emotions pass normative judgment on the normative judgments expressed by the first-order emotions to which they react. But it cannot be final judgment as in the case of volitions.

What a disapproving emotional response to one of one's own emotional responses represents is a judgment normatively critical of a normative judgment of ours, and can therefore not be said to automatically have the upper hand, and certainly not the final word as in the case of a second-order volition. An incongruous emotional response to an emotional response can at most be said to register a clash of normative commitments, rather than a univocal trumping of the latter by the former. Hence although layered, because they cannot be considered hierarchical,[10] second-order emotions are better served by analogy to Jaeggi's (mistaken) understanding of second-order volitions than by Frankfurt's original.

The clash of commitments attested to by a disapproving second-order emotion in a relatively stable and coherent person can be of two kinds. The simplest and most common form of normative contradiction pertains, as in Jaeggi's account, to differences of depth and authenticity that require normative prioritizing, as when a enjoying a clever joke clashes with our liberal principles, fear of ridicule with our moral obligations, or a fleeting infatuation with a deeper love. In all such cases an initial emotion is liable to be met by a second-order disapproving emotion as a form of self-rebuke. These are cases of conflicting commitments that are expressed by contrasting emotional responses, and resolved by a Jaeggi-type appeal to their relative normative depth and authenticity.[11] To repeat, though layered, the normative import of first-and second-order emotions does not pertain to a prior ranking. Nor is their prior ranking always apparent. We may bravely take a stand in accord with our higher principles, and respond with cowardly fear of the consequences. Other cases can be more ambiguous as is Sartre's example of regretting and feeling remorse for

---

[10] Except in the most obvious cases of a vulgar chuckle, sudden panic, or pang of jealousy one regrets and berates oneself for immediately.

[11] Taylor's notion of Hypergoods (1989, 62–75) captures these kinds of cases dramatically. A Taylorian Hypergood is one among the many goods one lives by whose "ranking makes [it] of supreme … and overriding importance" relative to the others (62). Taylor introduces Hypergoods to solve the problem of normative self-criticism discussed briefly above §5.4 n.17. For a critique of Taylor's solution, see Fisch (2017, 48–51).

abandoning an ailing relative to take up a pressing political or ethical cause. All these are cases of conflicting emotional responses that owe to conflicting normative commitments that can only be resolved by ranking them.

However, a conflicting second-order emotion can attest to more than a need for normative prioritizing. Far more significantly, it can be expressive of normative ambivalence—a state of mind of major consequence, as we have seen, for the very possibility of rational normative realignment. As I explained in the previous chapter, it is impossible for a person to hold her own normative commitments in critical check, because such a critical argument can never be levelled from her own perspective. And for that reason, we can never be convinced by such an argument when levelled at us by others. We can only do so when in a state of normative ambivalence toward the commitments in question. In previous work I have explored in some detail how and why normative criticism levelled at us by trusted others can have such an ambivalating effect on our commitment to the norms of ours they challenge, and have assumed that exposure to such external normative critique was the only rational form it could take (Fisch and Benbaji 2011, 254–271; Fisch 2017, 85–99). But thinking about second-order emotions in the present context, raises a different, and interesting option.

As we have seen, the destabilizing jolt by means of which normative criticism levelled from without is liable to have an ambivalating effect on its addressees' commitments owes to its apparent *un*truthfulness. To form such an argument necessarily requires attributing to its addressees norms to which they could not adhere. As a result, when exposed to external normative criticism we are implicitly presented with a portrayal of our I-part that diverges from our own self-image exactly with respect to those of our commitments our critics call into question. Faced by two jarring normative profiles, both supposedly our own, we are liable to be rendered ambivalent toward the norms in dispute. And because a person can never present herself with a critical argument whose premises diverge from what she takes her relevant commitments to be, one can never ambivalate oneself in this way, or so I thought.

A spontaneous emotional response to a turn of events can take us by surprise, and at times take us aback. And when unexpected, can be rewarded by an equally spontaneous second-order emotional reaction, which is also liable to take us by surprise and at times to take us aback. As I put it above, a surprising emotional response is a normative judgment coupled to a moment of self-discovery. If we are averse to certain types of behavior or afraid of dogs, we will not be surprised or taken aback by being suddenly angered by a case of the former or startled by the neighbors' golden retriever. Here it is the unanticipated type of behavior or the sudden appearance of the dog that startles us, not our emotional reaction. When surprised or taken aback by an emotional reaction we experience a moment of self-disclosure, as an evaluative disposition presents itself of which we had not been aware. Such moments can be more or less normatively consequential. Realizing, due to an unexpected visit, parting, or death, that our love ran deeper than we had imagined, can be overwhelming. It can also be worrying in the light of other pressing obligations we might have. Cases of the latter kind might call for normative prioritizing, but because neither

6.4 The Curious Status of Second-Order Emotions

case, surprising as they may be, implies a change or realignment of normative commitment, only a deepening or intensifying of an existing one, they will not have an ambivalating effect.

But when a sudden emotional response takes us aback—as when startled to find ourselves paralyzed by fear in a situation we'd long imagined braving, enjoying the kind of low bigoted humor we thought we despised, or jealous of our divorcee's new spouse—and we react to it negatively—annoyed by our sudden fear, woeful of enjoying the comedian's low humor, bewildered by feeling jealous—it could well be a sign of normative ambivalence. That a disapproving second-order emotional reaction can be expressive, and hence *symptomatic* of normative ambivalence and, hence, render us aware of being ambivalated, goes without saying. Like any form of undecidedness, it can be difficult to distinguish between truly being of two minds about a certain threat, another form of life, or a former spouse, and being merely confused or unclear about our true commitments. How to get ourselves right, as Frankfurt (2006) has it, is seldom an easy task, but my concern here is different. Can a startling emotional response that instigates an emotional reaction critical of it be, not only *indicative* of normative ambivalence, but could it actually *produce* it?

Focusing on the possible rationality of normative realignment (a question crucial to the study of scientific revolutions, for example), my former work had centered exclusively on the potentially ambivalating force of external normative criticism. Only when criticized from without, I argued, are we confronted by a normative framework resembling our own, yet different from it with respect to the norms it questions. And, again, the potentially ambivalating force of such critique owes not to its diversion from our *true* commitments, but from those we *deem* to be ours. Truth plays no role in the ambivalating process, only what the person criticized *takes to be* her true commitments. It is to this kind of discrepancy that a startling emotional response can also expose us.

Frankfurt focuses on getting ourselves right, as if our true self is some sort of a given about which we could be discernably right or wrong; to which our self-image might or might not be found to correspond. The notorious epistemological difficulties surrounding the very ideas of givenness and discernable correspondence, even with respect to our inner nature,[12] lie beyond the modest confines of the present work. Suffice it to say, first, that the normative framework relevant to how we judge ourselves and others, and central to our self-identity is the one we sincerely *believe* is ours. And, second, that the framework we believe to be ours at any given moment is dynamic and constantly changing in the light of new events, circumstances, and realizations.

An emotional reaction is a form of spontaneous, unthinking, yet cognitive, normative judgment. It can be wrong, but only by misconceiving its object. When we rage, rejoice, or are saddened by X we are reacting to what we take X to be, about which we may prove mistaken when realizing that X is not the frightening, happy or devastating state of affairs we mistook it to be. But an emotional reaction cannot be

---

[12] Of which Descartes believed our knowledge was impeccable and immune to skepticism.

mistaken with respect to the norm it brings to bear on X. In being spontaneous, an emotional reaction, one could say, is of itself proof of its normative authenticity. If X is indeed what we take it be, there seems to be no sense at all in accusing us of reacting mistakenly by responding angrily instead of happily. (We could be accused of being wrongly committed, but not of mistaking a bona fide commitment of ours for another.)

In other words, when we respond emotionally, the judgment we pass in doing so pertains to norms to which we are knowingly committed. If our emotional response takes us aback, it can only be because we were not aware of being so committed—fearful of X instead of bravely taking a stand, enjoying instead of despising X, etc. Of itself, however, surprise, even when unpleasant, does not constitute a normative judgment. But when an emotional response that takes us aback elicits a contrary, second-order emotional response, we have proof of an authentic internal normative clash.

Authentic, but not necessarily symmetrical. Both pertain to contrary normative judgments, each of which, in turn, to conflicting normative commitments. But it is the first-order response that by taking us by surprise attests to a significant change in what we took our I-part to be, while our second-order counter-response indicates, just as strongly, that it is a change to which we are normatively averse—and hence that we are either in need of a decisive priority check, or are experiencing genuine normative ambivalence.

In the latter case, the question of whether the quick succession of conflicting emotions we experience merely attests to our being normatively ambivalent, or can be said to have triggered it would seem to be inconsequential. In one sense it doesn't even arise. For once ambivalated and aware of it, resolving our two-mindedness takes precedence, regardless of whatever prompted it. But in a different, more philosophical sense, the question is important because it leads to a different one.

How we gain reliable self-knowledge is a thorny and long-debated question.[13] All agree, however, that we are never *fully* self-transparent. We can certainly harbor what Frankfurt terms volitional necessities unawares—namely, things we cannot and cannot but will ourselves to do in principle, which lacking the appropriate circumstances may remain forever hidden from us. Being Committed seems different. Because of the transitive nature of the verb, it seems incoherent to speak of being unconsciously committed. As noted above, taken aback by an emotional response attests to our being normatively committed unawares. But I shall leave open the question of the nature of the realization: whether such moments attest to the unanticipated *forming* of a commitment, as when falling in love, or to a tacit commitment rendered explicit. The important point for the present discussion is that, to repeat, our I-part, the seat of our norms and standards by which we pass conscious judgment on ourselves and others, pertains only to what we are *knowingly* committed,

---

[13] For a useful summary of, and engagement with recent work on self-knowledge and first-person authority see Byrne (2018) whose account of self-knowledge extends to desire and emotion (with special reference to disgust). Interestingly, like many he seems to subsume self-knowledge of one's normative commitments under that of one's beliefs.

6.4 The Curious Status of Second-Order Emotions

which is just another way of saying that we can knowingly pass judgment only on the basis of norms to which we are knowingly pledged. Therefore, although emotional responses are spontaneous, the norm-laden judgments they express must also pertain to our known commitments. From which follows that although there is always much to learn about our commitments known as tacit—as to what exactly they premise, what they entail, and how they relate to one another—just as one can only knowingly judge on the basis of known commitments, one cannot be unknowingly ambivalent toward one.

Commitments, explicit or tacit can be unknowingly inconsistent, unclear, or ambiguous. But only people can be ambivalent—not merely unsure about a commitment, but being incoherently of two minds about it. One can, therefore, be or become normatively ambivalated only toward components of one's operating I-part. One cannot be normatively ambivalent unawares. And because emotional responses are expressive, rather than constitutive of normative attitudes, if the quick succession of conflicting emotions we experience does indeed express normative ambivalation, the ambivalating factor has to be the happening X that prompted them.

Not unlike the potentially ambivalating effect of external normative criticism, a process of rational normative realignment, impossible to achieve by means of straightforward reflective deliberation no matter how self-critical, can thus also be set in motion by a disapproving second-order emotional reaction. Such normative two-mindedness demands resolution, which is achieved by subjecting the destabilized norm to the critical scrutiny of the ambivalated person's remaining commitments, which would not be possible otherwise. As a result the commitment in question will be either restored to its former I-part status, or demoted and replaced by another.

In this way, disapproving second-order emotions can have the same effect as the normatively disapproving critical arguments of people committed differently, thus extending the range of rational normative self-transformation. However, as I argued in the previous chapter, what renders partaking in the game of giving and asking for reasons the epitome of rationality is the realization (a) that to be committed to a norm *rationally*, requires subjecting it to normative self-critique, which is possible only in a state of normative ambivalence, and (b) that, because such a state can be achieved by exposing that commitment to the normative critique of others. Actively seeking such critique for that reason represents human rationality at its absolute best.

But to what extent, we can now ask, can one, for the same reason, actively seek to become normatively ambivalated by the "come again" effect of a second-order emotional reaction? Both successive emotional reactions are spontaneous and, unlike engaging the reasons game, cannot be undertaken voluntarily. There is nothing even remotely rational or contrived, i.e. done for a reason, in genuine emotional reactions per se. But is there a sense in which a person can be said to deliberately precipitate an emotional "come-again" effect for reasons analogous to joining the reasons game? Normative ambivalence is a necessary and sufficient condition for normative self-critique, but there are no necessary or sufficient conditions for *becoming* normatively ambivalent. Exposing oneself to the normative critique of others is liable, but by no means is it guaranteed to have an ambivalating effect.

Similarly, formerly imagined, though never yet experienced circumstances are liable, but are by no means guaranteed to set off an emotional "come again" effect. And these, not unlike entering a critical conversation with others, can be rationally sought out and explored.

Rorty (1989) argues insistently against the very possibility of reasoned normative realignment (or of rationally modifying or replacing one's "final vocabulary", as he has it[14]), on the grounds that a normative framework (or final vocabulary) cannot be normatively criticized from within. The hero of his account, the "strong poet", whose image he portrays and promotes, and with whom he fully identifies,[15] is someone who knowingly conducts herself fully aware of this constraint on her rationality. She, therefore:

(1) … has radical and continuing doubts about the final vocabulary she currently uses ...; (2) She realizes that arguments phrased in her present vocabulary can neither underwrite nor dissolve these doubts; (3) Insofar as she philosophizes about her situation, she does not think that her vocabulary is closer to reality[16] than others, that it is in touch with a power not herself. (73)

She is portrayed as self-critical, but only in the sense of tracing the outer-borders of self-criticism. Aware of her final vocabulary's inherent contingency, she doubts it persistently, and spends "her time worrying about the possibility that she has been initiated into the wrong tribe, taught to play the wrong language game." However, and this is Rorty's crucial point, "she cannot give a criterion of wrongness", and thinks, therefore, that there "is no reason to think that Socratic inquiry into the essence of justice or science or rationality will take one much beyond the language games of one's time."(74–5).

Rorty's strong poet, therefore, trades propriety for novelty, experimenting with new vocabularies by blindly casting around for new metaphors to redescribe herself and her world. Unable to question, she dabbles; unable to criticize, she tinkers, groping blindly, because she assumes, with Rorty, that from the vantage point of her current vocabulary—which is the only committed vantage point available to her—it is impossible to articulate what might be wrong with it, or in what ways it might be improved. Rorty's ironist certainly aims to *improve* upon her vocabulary, rather than merely change it for another, but is unable to set herself a prospective goal; other than to change for the sake of change. She cannot, therefore, envisage progress. Rorty insists that the main incentive for all manner of creative reform boils down to fear of unoriginality, thus radically extending Harold Bloom's notion of the driving

---

[14] The position to which I refer, is developed in the first two chapters of Rorty (1989), with which I deal in detail in Fisch & Benbaji (2011, ch.1).

[15] Sliding effortlessly between reference to "the ironist" and "we ironists". See for example pp. 79–81.

[16] When the focus is on normative commitment rather than factual belief, as in the present essay, closeness to reality is beside the point. Commitment to a norm is to a standard of propriety or rightness. There is nothing wrong in being wholeheartedly committed to the ideas, people, social and political frameworks, forms of art and forms of life one cherishes while fully acknowledging that others are liable to be committed to radically different ones. Reality has nothing to do with it.

force of the "anxiety of influence" from poetry to all forms of rational improvement.[17] To remain original, the strong poet must view her final vocabulary ironically, and keep telling her story differently, blindly redescribing with the hope of hitting unwittingly upon an option that in retrospect she will find worthwhile.

To this end, and with a view of expanding their range of options beyond those they are capable of imagining, he urges creative individuals to experience and experiment with forms of life different from their own with the hope of being won over by a different set of commitments from which, looking back on their former way of thinking, they would deem it a step forward.

Rorty replaces rationality with irony. He is right in claiming that no one, creative or imaginative as she may be, can normatively criticize the normative framework to which she is committed merely by talking to herself. It is safe to assume, I think, that he would have made an exception for cases of normative ambivalence, although he nowhere raises the subject. Unfortunately, the image of the fiercely original and independent "strong poet" on which he models all framework transitions, blinds him to the transformative ambivalating potential of *dialogue* with others, and hence to the rationality of seeking their criticism proactively.[18] However, it has become apparent that when thought of in terms of its ambivalating potential, rather than a mere broadening of horizons, Rorty's strong poet's proactive experimentation with other forms of life represents a higher form of rationality Rorty believed was impossible.

Bibliography

Bloom H (1973) The anxiety of influence: a theory of poetry. Oxford University Press, Oxford
Brandom RB (2000) Articulating reasons: an introduction to inferentialism. Harvard University Press, Cambridge, MA
Brandom RB (2009) Reason in philosophy: animating ideas. Harvard University Press, Cambridge, MA
Byrne A (2018) Transparency and self-knowledge. Oxford University Press, Oxford
Fisch M (2017) Creatively undecided: toward a history and philosophy of scientific agency. University of Chicago Press, Chicago
Fisch M (2020) Talmudic commentary and the problem of normative self-critique. Geschichte der Philologien 57(58):27–43
Fisch M, Benbaji Y (2011) The view from within: normativity and the limits of self-criticism. University of Notre Dame Press, South Bend
Frankfurt HG (2004) The reasons of love. Princeton University Press, Princeton
Frankfurt HG (2006) Taking ourselves seriously and getting it right. Stanford University Press, Stanford
Jaeggi R (2014) Alienation (trans: Neuhauser F, Smith AE). Columbia University Press, New York

---

[17] Bloom (1973). For his reference to Bloom see Rorty (1989, 24–25).

[18] See Fisch (2020) for the one large-scale intellectual undertaking I know that explicitly adopts such a form of non-Socratic dialogical engagement as its master norm.

Kant I (1999) Critique of pure reason (trans: Guyer P, Wood AW). Cambridge University Press, Cambridge

Korsgaard CM (2009) Self-constitution: agency, identity, and integrity. Oxford University Press, Oxford

Rorty R (1989) Contingency, irony, solidarity. Cambridge University Press, Cambridge

Taylor G (1985) Pride, shame and guilt. Oxford University Press, Oxford

Taylor C (1989) Sources of the self: the making of the modern identity. Harvard University Press, Cambridge, MA

Chapter 7
All Together Now

Abstract After discussing the four orders of reflexive emotion separately, this chapter places them side by side, with a view to showing, first, that in addition to being exclusively human, each of them constitutes a profound manifestation of a different grounding component of our humanity: primary shame, of the most rudimentary aspect of human selfhood; secondary shame, of our normativity; humor, of the uniqueness of our conceptual languages; humility, of our very rationality; second-order emotions, of our ability rationally assess our normative commitments. Second, setting them side by side allows us to appreciate the extent to which living up to our full human potential necessarily requires engaging real others—a claim of crucial political significance.

Keywords Primary shame · Secondary shame · Adam and eve · Cain and Abel · Birth of self · Birth of normativity · I-part · Humor · Conceptual language · Conceptual failure · Humility · Value of otherness · Open society · John Rawls · Political liberalism · Tower of babel

7.1 Introduction

The emotions do not rank high in comparison to humankind's loftier faculties and cognitive endowments, even among cognitivists. In view of their spontaneous, unconsidered, and involuntary nature, the unreasoned motivating force they exert, their fierce subjectivity, and many parallels and anticipations in other animals, they are considered a distrustful form of judgment better overseen and held in check by more thoughtful, detached modes of evaluation. Thus, the lion's share of master cognitivist Martha Nussbaum's extended emotions work is devoted to how to protect society from the negative effects of such otherwise valuable emotions as fear,

© The Author(s), under exclusive license to Springer Nature
Switzerland AG 2025
M. Fisch, *Reflexive Emotions*, SpringerBriefs in Philosophy,
https://doi.org/10.1007/978-3-031-83764-7_7

shame, disgust and anger.[1] Our emotions, all agree, even those considered negative, all have positive functions, at least in marking, by their very spontaneity, what we are really attracted to, recoil from, rejoice in, and saddened by, or in short, marking for us and to an extent for others who we really are, behind our veils of self-control.

But even here, in the realm of what they can teach us better than any other inward or outward mode of expression, the emotions retain a keen individuality, limiting what they can teach us to the personal make-up of those who have them. And yet, if there is any truth in what has emerged so far, this study joins a small body work[2] that views certain reflexive emotions as pointedly indicative, not of what makes their individual bearers special, but of the very nature of our shared humanity—even more than our loftier endowments.

7.2 Shame Again

To recapitulate. The kind of primary shame experienced when exposed to a peeping Tom or to an intimate medical examination by an imposter teaches us much about the very topography of human selfhood and the rudimentary form of agency required to secure and maintain the self's outer boundaries.

Primary shame attests to the most basic form of the human split self, with one, agential part of us granted the authority to oversee and safeguard what we deem to be private and hence ours in the most elementary sense of the term: the privacy of our thoughts, our feelings, and our bodies. These are so elementally ours that, unlike our abodes and possessions, that merely *belong* to us, our thoughts, feelings and bodies are in a deep sense, not merely ours, but *us*! Moreover, it is up to us, and to us alone, to draw the line between private and public in this regard, first, quite generally, and then, more individually with respect to specific people. The norms of modesty, honesty, openness, and restraint at work in how we dress and express ourselves in the company of others are largely social. We comply with them as a matter of course but at times choose not to. Yet, whether obeying or defying our society's accepted norms of self-presentation, if we are not coerced, it is always us who willfully do so.

Our thoughts, feelings and bodies are self-defining. But it is our ability to actively choose which of our thoughts, feelings and what of our bodies to reveal and to hide from the rest of society that renders us human agents; creatures not merely *propelled* by the demands of their bodies and what they know and feel, and the demands of society on them, but fully-fledged agents capable of stepping back from them and drawing and safeguarding the line between which of them we are willing to reveal,

---

[1] See especially Nussbaum (2004, 2010, 2012, 2016, 2018).

[2] Among them Halbertal on primary and secondary shame, Nussbaum on what she terms primitive shame, Bergson and Schopenhauer on humor, referred to in previous chapters.

7.2 Shame Again

and to whom, and which we are adamant to keep to ourselves. Part of what we are determined to hide, are thoughts, feelings and bodily attributes we'd have preferred not to have. But, contrary to Nussbaum's notion of primitive shame,[3] the economy of privacy, of keeping part of ourselves to ourselves, is for the most part not at all motivated by self-disapproval or self-disappointment, but by a deep-set desire for self-*definition* and self-*positioning*.

A country's very coherence, to take an obvious analogy, depends on it not only having clear borders, but having the exclusive authority to maintain and secure them from within. Regardless of its dependency on others, a state's very integrity, autonomy and individuality depends, first and foremost, on its ability to maintain and control its boundaries. And the same goes for individual selfhood. The ability to stand back, take stock, and respond to ourselves (not only to our first-order volitions, as Frankfurt has it, but of the sum-total of our bodily attributes, thoughts, and feelings)—in addition to standing back, taking stock, and responding to our surroundings, an ability we share with other animals—is the defining feature of human selfhood and agency. However, as with statehood, selfhood and agency assert themselves not in the *ability* to stand back from ourselves, but in *assuming the responsibility* and *exercising the authority* to do so; in viewing self-critique and self-government as fundamental duties, as matters of personal normative commitment. And as in the case of statehood, the most elemental act of self-government is that of autonomously setting, safeguarding, and managing the boundaries of the self itself.

And, again, as in the case of statehood, managing the boundaries of the self amounts to much more than keeping ourselves to ourselves to the exclusion of all others. As we have seen, maintaining the boundaries of the human self involves managing a multi-dimensional network of special relationships with people whom we grant different levels of access to the privacy of our thoughts, feelings and bodies; a self-controlled economy of intimacy and closeness constitutive of our self-positioning as members of the social spheres we inhabit and interact with.

Delineating, safeguarding, and managing the private realm of our thoughts, feelings, and bodies are norm-laden acts of agency conducted on the basis of what we deem to be *best* kept hidden, and to whom, if at all, we deem it, nonetheless, *fitting* to reveal. However, as I noted above, there is a categorical difference between the thoughts, feelings and physical attributes we keep hidden because we deem them private, and what we hide because we consider them wrong or inappropriate. Primary shame pertains to an act of agency that *precedes* taking normative stock *of* our thoughts, actions and bodies; it pertains to the thoughts feelings and bodily attributes we deem to be private and to share with a precious few, because we see them as comprising our core self, not because we'd rather not have had them.

The self-determination of the core self we deem ourselves to be is a norm-laden, yet non-judgmental act of agency that logically precedes standing back from ourselves to determine who we *want to be*, or would rather be, which is a norm-laden

---

[3] See above Sect. 3.2.

self-judgmental act of agency that only a self-determined self can undertake. Primary shame is experienced when the self's self-determined boundaries are deliberately breached by uninvited transgressors; a reflexive, self-directed emotional response to having failed to safeguard and maintain the self's very integrity. Secondary shame, by contrast, responds to a categorically different form of self-failing: failure to live up to whom we *want* to be.

7.2.1 A Biblical Interlude

Many people read the Bible's description the birth of humanity as we know it as a moment of confusing conflation of primary and secondary shame. As if upon eating from tree of the knowledge of good and evil (Gen. 2:17) Adam and Eve experienced both primary shame for being naked and secondary shame for having sinned. But a closer look at the text reveals that their initial reaction after eating the forbidden fruit is carefully related only to the former. Before eating from the tree, we are told they were naked, yet did not feel shame (2:25), and we may safely assume that by the same token, they also proceeded cluelessly oblivious to the difference between good and evil. Upon eating from it, we are told, "their eyes opened and they knew they were naked", and to cover their nakedness sewed "fig leaves together and made themselves loincloths" (3:7). But of being ashamed for having sinned, not a word!

Even later, when asked rhetorically by God why they had hidden themselves after hearing "His voice in the garden", the man's answer relates only to his nakedness, not to having sinned (3: 8–10). And God's response, like the text itself, also supports the idea that eating from the tree caused them only primary shame: "Who told thee that thou wast naked? Hast thou eaten from the tree, of which I commanded thee that thou shouldst not eat?" (3:11).

What I believe the text strongly implies, is that choosing to obey or disobey even a firm divine command, does not require an ability to distinguish right from wrong in the normative sense of terms. Obedience per se is a matter of utility, or preference, not of propriety; of what Taylor calls weak, rather than strong evaluation. Animals lacking any notion of propriety can be trained to obey instructions at the risk of being punished, which they are liable to disobey when paying the price seems worth it. Disobedience as such is not a *normative* failure to be ashamed of, but, at most, a miscalculation. Eating from tree, the text implies, rendered the first humans *capable* of becoming moral agents, capable of committing to standards of propriety, of knowing good from evil, not by fitting them with ready-made norms and standards, but by rendering them human selves, agents capable of self-delineation and self-determination, and hence of primary shame. Normativity, as we shall see in a moment. Will come later. With Cain.

First, however, to an aspect of the first phase in the Bible's perceptive account of the birth of humanity, which to the best of my knowledge has so far gone unnoticed. If, as the text seems clearly to imply, Adam and Eve's shame of being naked should be seen as a case of primary, rather than secondary shame, with no one else yet to share their world, from whose gaze, we must ask, were the newly enlightened Adam and Eve trying to conceal their nakedness? Surely not from one another. Who then was the cause of their primary shame? When Adam and Eve first become aware of their nakedness it seems clearly that it is from God that they shamefully conceal it and from His gaze attempt to hide, which raises an unsettling thought.

To live under the constant scrutinizing gaze of a God who "tests the mind and the heart" (Jer. 11:20), who looks not merely "at the outward appearance", as do we, "but ... at the heart" (Sam 16:7), is to live, robbed of one's privacy, in a perpetual Times-Square-news-ribbon, nightmarish state of total transparency. God commands total intimacy, which, because enforced, and never freely granted, is self-obliterating. Eating from the tree, before anything normative has been learnt or experienced—except for fearing the consequences of their disobedience, which, as noted, is not particularly human—vividly represents the very birth of human selfhood—humankind's defining difference from all other creature. But it does so conjoined with Adam and Eve's worrying realization of divine omniscience. With no third human party yet in existence, they shamefully cover their nakedness in a vain and futile attempt to assert their newly found selfhood in the self-effacing conditions of total exposure to God's all-seeing, all-knowing gaze.

Viewed thus, eating from the forbidden Tree not only marks the dramatic birth of humankind's primary shame, and with it that of the autonomous human self, but at the same time lays bare the fundamental paradox of the Bible's religious anthropology. That although created autonomous and free-willed, their Lord Creator's very omniscience inevitably robs humankind of its most basic form of personal autonomy and self-constitution: the freedom to the privacy of one's self, and the authority to define, safeguard and control it.

7.2.2 A Second Biblical Interlude

According to the biblical narrative, the birth of normativity itself, by which I mean the moment when the first humans became normative agents: committed to standards of propriety to which they held themselves and others accountable, as opposed to acquiring the *ability* in principle to become one (by eating from the tree), occurs later, in the aftermath of Abel's death at the hand of his brother.

Cain's killing of Abel was not the first murder, but the birth of murder. In all of animal kingdom the struggle for survival and reproduction is often a struggle to the death, as was the two brothers' fervent jostling for divine attention and favor. Cain, it is fair to assume, could not have known better, just as we can just as fairly assume that God was well aware that by shunning Cain's sacrifice and favoring Abel's He had put Abel in mortal danger. And yet God makes no attempt to save Abel's life, as He would save Isaac from his father's hand.

God's exchanges with Cain, both before and after the killing, read as profoundly didactic, designed not to punish a transgression, so much as to cause Cain to realize that he had breached a normative boundary of which he was not yet aware, yet should be. Cain, we are told, was angered by the rejection of his sacrifice (4:5). "Why art thou angry?" enquired the Lord, feigning innocent curiosity, "why art thou crestfallen?" If you will do good[4] you shall be accepted, and if not you shall be slave to sin (4:6). Urged to do the right thing, Cain then kills his brother, which the text clearly implies seemed to him to be the right thing to do!

Cain's brash and dismissive 'how should I know?' response to God's rhetorical question "Where is Abel thy brother?" (4:9) shows no regret or panic at having done anything wrong. Nor does he try to hide from God. He certainly does not seem ashamed. If anything, his rude answer implicitly acknowledges God's omniscience, as if saying 'you know very well where he is". This, I suggest, is not because Cain was a heartless and ruthless murderer. He truly thought that he was following God's advice to do the right thing. And when God finally responds, He does not admonish Cain for disobeying a divine command, for no such command had been issued. Nor does God call Cain to task to reprimand him for violating a norm of which he should have been aware, if not committed to. What God does do is to firmly express His displeasure with what Cain had done, cursing the earth for him (4:11–12) (not unlike his father (3:17–19)), and banishing him from the agricultural life of his choosing, to roam the land as a fugitive. God refrains from punishing Cain measure for measure, by demanding a life for a life, blood for blood, as His command later to Noah and his family, prohibiting human bloodshed clearly instructs: "Whoso sheds man's blood by man shall his blood be shed; for in the image of God made he man" (9:6). On the contrary. God marks Cain "lest any finding him should smite him" (4:15). Cain was to start anew by first wandering the land and spreading the word.

By registering His displeasure and informing Cain that his brother's spilt blood cries to him from the ground, God causes Cain to realize that he had done wrong; not to have disobeyed but to have done *wrong*. For Cain is presented as the first human being who, after internalizing the gravity of his deed, shamefully declares "Too great is my sin to bear!" (4:13),[5] and to go on immediately to brood over the horror of his crime becoming common knowledge.

> Behold, thou hast driven me out this day from the face of the earth; and from thy face I shall be hid; and I shall be a fugitive and a vagabond in the earth; and it shall come to pass, that anyone that finds me shall slay me (4:14)

The word shame is not used here, but the futile image of attempting to hide from God is, and with it the Biblical narrative's first and constitutive moment of normative self-admonishment—the quintessential form of secondary shame. As I noted, Cain is banished from his land, and forced to take to the road, to reinvent himself while wandering, and marked by God, to promulgate his newly found normativity among the first human settlers, who by the end of the chapter had claimed God's world as a template for the creation of their human world with its art and industry

---

[4] And not "do well", as most English translation render the Hebrew "*im teitiv*".

[5] And not "Too great is my *punishment* to bear" as for some reason virtually all English translations render the biblical "*gadol avoni minso*".

7.2 Shame Again   83

and variety of life forms (4:20–26). Cain himself, we are told founded the first urban settlement (17).

And thus, if eating from the tree represents the birth of Halbertalian human self-hood, and with it, the alarming awakening of being forever exposed to God's accusing gaze, Cain's killing of Abel represents the birth of human normativity, and with it, the alarming realization of being forever exposed to *one's own* accusing gaze.

7.2.3 The Inner Self

Shame isn't funny, neither primary nor secondary. Painful self-failings never are. And yet torturing ourselves when our boundaries are violated, and castigating ourselves for falling short of whom we aspire to be constitute emotional moments of self-disapproval through which our very humanity shines forth. One of the several things not mentioned so far that mark us off from any other animal or artificial intelligence is a unique ability to dislike ourselves. Self-disapproval comes in a variety of forms some less interesting than others. At the lowest rung are cases of self-discontent born of jealousy of other people's real or imagined endowments or accomplishments, which, because wholly unattainable, cannot begin to motivate self-correction. Such unrealistic escapist fantasies can be fun, but when taken seriously can have a depressing incapacitating effect. There's a world of difference between pressing self-critique into the service of reasoned, rational self-corrective action, and refusing to accept oneself to the point of despair.[6]

Situated a few rungs higher is envy of achievable endowments and accomplishments that motivates realistic self-improvement. Inspiring role-models, real and imagined, play an important role in every phase of our lives. They set us achievable standards by means of living or lifelike examples for whom and what we could become if willing to invest the effort. I term this a form of jealousy or envy despite the negative connotations of the terms,[7] because the standards our role models set us are external. Jealousy is not a reflexive emotion. It requires an external object to do its work, positive or negative.

It is when standards set for us by others are internalized and rendered personal commitments, that we begin to measure ourselves against wholly internal yard-sticks, which, in turn, render the emotions produced by measuring ourselves against them, wholly reflexive too. When that happens, the emotions of jealousy and envy give way to an internally motivating resolve. In holding ourselves accountable to our own norms and values, proudly congratulating ourselves when we succeed and shamefully chastising ourselves when we do not, the exclusively human inner

---

[6] Which steers very close to Nussbaum's notion of primitive shame.

[7] Although they are employed positively on occasion, as in the Talmudic saying that "the jealousy of scribes increaseth wisdom" (Babylonian Talmud, *Bava Batra* 22a), and the late Krister Stendhal' well-known notion of "holy envy".

dialogue of the self-governing self asserts itself in a bewildering splitting of personhood.[8]

Who is one referring to in the first person when one declares to oneself that "I can't allow myself to do this, yet I can't help myself—what should I do?" Earlier in this essay, I introduced the useful Frankfurtian distinction between a person's empirical self and what I called her I-part as a way of differentiating between the thinking and acting self, and its norm-laden self-conscious overseer. But in the sentence above the self-referring, first-person "I"s and "myself"s seem to shift speaker between the two mid-sentence. The only coherent reading of such a statement is to relate all first-person attributions to the I-part speaker's thus: I (the I-part) cannot allow my empirical self to do this. Yet it (the empirical self) insists, and I (the I-part) cannot help it. What should I (the I-part) do? Read thus, it is our I-part, the seat of our norms and standards, expressing our second-order volitions, that is doing all the judging in an effort to coax our empirical self to toe the normative line. The beauty and uniqueness of human selfhood hence lies in how we identify ourselves in the first-person, not with whom we are, or happen to be, but with whom we believe we *ought* to be; with whom we desire and imagine ourselves becoming.

In other words, we locate ourselves in the first-person in the privacy of our innermost second-order desires, which, to do the work of guiding our normative inner dialogue effectively, must remain hidden from the eyes of all but those most close to us, and even they will never enjoy full access. What other people see and deem to be us is our empirical self, the self they observe in action, and with whom they interact, while the self we represent to ourselves in the first person hidden form the public eye, is our I-part, the self we aspire to be. Viewed thus, the capacity and exclusive authority to draw and control the line between the public and the private I (outwardly signified by exercising our absolute right to determine what of our bodies to reveal and to whom) is definitive of our very selfhood. Hence the profound sense of self-failing we experience when that line is deliberately violated. This is why primary shame is primary.

Secondary shame is the self-failing of an intact and properly functioning self. It is experienced when our empirical self fails to live up to our I-part's normative dictate. Secondary shame reflects the workings of a robust I-part whose failure to motivate its empirical counterpart to do the right thing does not reflect a weakness or lack of resolve on its part. On the contrary, the deeper the shame, the deeper the commitment to the unheeded norm. And same goes for primary shame. The deeper the offence, the firmer and more robust is the boundary violated. Schematically speaking, it is our empirical self that experiences secondary shame for failing to live up to its I-part's standards, or to those of the external or internalized witnesses to his failure. The two forms of shame are reflexive emotions that attest to much more than our ability to turn an inquisitive gaze inwards in self-conscious awareness of our thoughts, desires and feelings and react emotionally. The two forms of shame attest,

---

[8] Which, as noted above (Sect. 3.3.3) is sorely missing from Bernard Williams's account of shame.

in their very reflexivity, to the grounds, structure and dynamics of the human self itself in its intriguing two-tieredness.

7.2.4 The Joke's on Us

Shame is a dark emotion that bristles with remorse, self-blame, and self-reckoning. Humor, on the neo-Schopenhauerian showing presented here, is very different. Although it attests, like shame, to a self-failing, or at least to an unavoidable inner discordance, the emotion to which it gives rise is a major form of enjoyment, that can on occasion be quite uninhibited, yet will never give rise to self-reproach.[9] Like shame, humor also pertains to normativity, but of a different kind than shame. Humor also responds to a different kind of human failing than shame: to failings of self-expression, rather than to failings of self-constitution or self-government. Humor's reflexive focal point, as we have seen, are failings of human language, or, to use Brandom's cogent term, to those of human "concept mongering" (1994, xi).

Because we enjoy a good joke, humor might seem to attest to a less weighty sort of self-failing than the more harrowing two forms of shame. But it does not. Humor, I have argued, is expressive of an inherent, tragically inevitable, human failing, which because inescapable and all-pervading, is not experienced as a personal failing, or self-betrayal as is shame. Yet it goes to the heart of an even more basic aspect of our humanity, no less unique than human selfhood, and on which the well-functioning of the self and much more centrally depend. Only humans are capable of maintaining a functional two-tiered self as described, just as only humans, as argued in Chap. 4, can appreciate a joke. However, our ability to find a joke funny is evidence of an equally unique, yet far more significant exclusively human linguistic capacity that Schopenhauer keenly described.

As Taylor argues, for a functioning human I-part to perform its evaluative work, to judge, settle on maxims, criticize their implementation or lack of, and hold the self accountable, a vocabulary of identity informing normative concepts is required to render its commitments explicit. Putting our second-order desires in words is what allows us not merely to state what we want to want, but to reason with them and from them to determine, in Brandom's terms, to what else they further commit and entitle us.

We are 'language animals', as Taylor (2016) puts it, before we can be human selves, simply because to achieve human selfhood requires a capacity for human, that is to say, *conceptual* language. However, our linguistic capacity in general far transcends that of our capacity for normative self-interpretation.[10] First and foremost it is by means of our conceptual vocabularies that we represent the objects and states of affairs we sense and imagine, remember the ones we sensed and imagined

---

[9] Except perhaps for an amused, thigh slapping "how didn't I think of that before?"

[10] I am again alluding to Taylor; this time to his "Self-Interpreting Animals" (1985a, 45–76).

in the past and those we envisage sensing and imagining in the future. The limits of our conceptual vocabulary, as Wittgenstein famously puts it, mark the limits of our perceived, imagined and envisaged world.[11] But, if Schopenhauer's theory of the ludicrous can teach us anything, it is that the world we inhabit far transcends the linguistically determined limits of the world we perceive, imagine and envisage; that time and again the world we inhabit flies in the face of our conceptually impoverished attempts to properly represent it.

The world we inhabit comprises entities[12] and states of affairs that bear resemblance to one another while remaining in innumerous respects wholly unique.[13] We negotiate our world by applying what we learn from past experience to the present and the future, by reasoning from one state of affairs to another, by critically deliberating options before settling on one, and so forth. For a language to support such inferential, ampliative and eliminative reasoning; to enable statements about particular entities or states of affairs to have consequences for others, its vocabulary must be conceptual, namely, both general and inferentially connected. As argued in Chap. 4, elements of a conceptual vocabulary (as opposed to a vocabulary comprising only names or tags) designate kinds, natural or artificial, rather than single objects. They apply to particular objects by virtue of deeming them members of the classes of objects they represent or with reference to a class-defining exemplar. To judge a particular object to be a city, an insect, a contract, or a parent, is to *classify* it as a member of the class of cities, insects, contracts, or parents.

Concepts thus carve the world they purport to represent into an array of classes or kinds that stand to one another in complex relations of full and partial inclusion and exclusion that generate an inferential network of logical and material relations,[14] that supports the full range of reflective human judgment, deliberation and discourse. But it can only work if the unique singular features of whatever we are referring to are ignored in favor of whatever it has in common with members of the various classes of entities and state of affairs to which it is purported to belong.

---

[11] "The limits of my language mean the limits of my world" Wittgenstein (1922, §5.6).

[12] Including, of course, forms of life, ideas, opinions, speech acts, attitudes, laws and regulations, theories, cultures, as well as all the other non-material entities that furnish our world.

[13] This applies to what Sellars (1962) terms the "manifest image" of our world. What he calls the "scientific image" is not the world we experience and live in, but reality as envisaged when the physical sciences are taken as ontologically foundational. As Sellars admits, it is impossible, in principle, to represent the manifest image in terms of the scientific image as it now stands, certainly when its non-material ontology is factored in (although he did harbor the hope that one day it might). The point being that the scientific image comprises fundamental physical elements—particles, fields, forms of energy, strings, etc.—that are deemed to be absolutely identical, and hence fully expressible in the conceptual languages of physics and chemistry.

[14] The logical relations obtain by virtue of the formal class properties of inclusion and exclusion (siblings might also be parents, cannot be only children, and must share at least one parent). Material inferences pertain not to the formalities of a concept's extension, but to its content, such as the inference from 'Pittsburgh is to the west of Princeton' to 'Princeton is to the east of Pittsburgh', or from 'Lightening is seen now' to 'Thunder will be heard soon', to take two of Brandom's examples (Brandom (2000, 52).)

7.2 Shame Again

There is no such thing as a concept of a specific city or contract. When a concept's extension is narrowed to a single entity it becomes an ungeneralizable name or tag. A rich enough conceptual vocabulary can pinpoint particular referents (e.g. the person in the fifth row who asked the second question after this evening's talk), but the more specific the description, the less generalizable it necessarily becomes. To support reasoned discourse and deliberation, judgments of specific objects and states of affairs must remain sufficiently general, and therefore necessarily inaccurate. The inevitably built-in discrepancies between the objects we have in mind and their linguistic representations can be mild and insignificant to the inferential task in hand, but weight is relative to context and is presupposed of it.

Be this as it may, what is always necessarily sacrificed in every linguistic rendering, is precisely what makes its object special and hence worthy of our attention. This is why articulation, though indispensable for all our reasoning, can never fully achieve its representative goals, and will forever present us with pale, shallow and overly schematic depictions of what we are trying to discuss. It is a shortcoming of articulation as such, which can be as fatal or detrimental as it can be trivial or insignificant; a shortcoming that is due not to faulty concepts, but to the very nature of conception itself, and as such, constitutes an all-pervading and inevitable failing of our rational selves themselves.

Concepts, of course, can be deemed faulty, and be replaced or modified,[15] they can be narrowed down and better tailored to the specifics of specific objects, but *qua* concepts they will *necessarily* remain general, and will, therefore, be necessarily prone to misconceive the particular objects they are designated to represent. Rationality requires conception, and conception necessarily generates a measure of misconception. Therefore, all rational endeavor, because of its reliance on our linguistic capacity, harbors the possibility of its own undoing, relative, not to the nominal, to reality in itself, as it were, but to the phenomenal, to reality as humanly experienced in its immediate richness.[16]

Such misconceptions can be anything but funny. (These lines were first drafted during the tragic aftermath of Israel's colossal failures of conception of October 7th, 2023.) Joking, though, is playful. What we humorously present and appreciate as comical knowingly plays in ironic amusement on largely inconsequential failures of conception that harbor no collateral damage. The greater the failure, the more unanticipated, the more apparent in retrospect, the better the joke. Jokes are made to catch one out. They present a compelling conception, which is then abruptly exploded, their concrete subject-matter always victorious. We might enjoy discovering conceptual failures that go in the opposite direction, as when a concept is found to apply to cases we'd rather it didn't, or not to apply to cases we'd rather it did. Much legislation work is about closing potential legal loopholes by redefining

---

[15] Although, as the diversified and swiftly expanding literature on conceptual engineering amply proves, how to conceive concept amelioration as a reasoned process is far from straight forward.

[16] Worse still when concepts are envisioned, not for what they are, flat, generic depictions of a class of objects' common denominator or paradigmatic exemplar, but delusionally, as representing their very ideal platonic essence.

legal concepts. Imre Lakatos made much of what he called "monster-adjustment" and "monster-barring" in the dialectic process of articulating mathematical theorems and proving them.[17] Such cases might strike us as mildly entertaining, but we don't find them funny.

What we do find funny is when we are abruptly made to realize that we're lost for a word we were sure we had. Joking preys on cases of unharmful, yet acute conceptual muteness, fooling us to put an inadequate concept confidently to work only to find it laughably inappropriate. Viewed thus, our gleeful reaction to what we find funny is a reflexive emotion par excellence, though very different from shame.

In the case of shame, we are also reacting to a discrepancy between a concept (honesty, fairness, bravery, consideration, modesty), to which we are committed, and a specific state of affairs within its domain. But when ashamed, it is not the concept we shamefully fault, but our conduct, to which it should have been applied. By contrast, when we laugh, what is gleefully faulted is the concept we firmly believed should have applied to the state of affairs that is found to rudely fly in its face. Both judgments, faulting our conduct for falling short of a norm of conduct to which we are committed, and faulting a conceptual norm to which we are committed for failing in its representative duties, are passed by what Schopenhauer calls our rational self, and I, our I-part. In the former judgment our I-part calls our empirical self to task, in the latter, it admits its own failing in a gleeful display of self-irony. This is as close as our I-part can get to self-critique unassisted. Appreciating a joke does not add up to a reasoned, prospective act of normative critique. It is more a retroactive act of recognizing a failure after the event. But it is not a moment of grudging confession, but one of gleeful delight at having learnt something we could never teach ourselves.

This is a point worth dwelling on. We often surprise ourselves in awakening abruptly to a misconceiving on our part. When consequential, we might experience alarm or frustration. But when not, we might smile, even chuckle in amusement. But such self-discoveries never amount to telling ourselves a joke. A good joke knowingly contrives to take us by surprise; to fool us into adopting a conception which it goes on to be curtly exploded. We can remember a joke, but cannot tell ourselves one. Intentional laughter is a reflexive emotion. Although what we are reacting to is a conceptual self-failing, finding something funny is a form of self-critique that requires a *dialogical* setting. We need to be told the joke (vocally or in writing), and to experience the conceptual failing with a jolt. It won't be funny if it's explained to us. For a joke to be funny, realizing the conceptual failure has to be unforeseen and abrupt, but not the dialogical setting. We can come fully prepared to be taken aback, pay for a ticket to see a comedian or a comedy, ask to be told a joke, and so forth. In such situations we know, and are fully prepared to being fooled. What needs to be wholly unanticipated is the punchline. And punchlines can only be delivered by somebody else. When nothing substantial is at stake, we enjoy being led by the nose and caught out and off guard by a good joke. We also emerge from

---

[17] Lakatos (1976). See also Buzaglo (2001).

it the wiser; better aware of the extension of the conceptual norm that failed; no longer as easily fooled with respect to it.

Differently from shame, however, our unique ability to enjoy a joke, brings out, if only in rudimentary form, an additional dimension of our humanity that concerns the limits of normative self-criticism, and the indispensable role of others in breaching them—a point central to our discussion of humility.

7.3 In My Humble Opinion

What shame and humor have in common is humankind's most exclusive capacity: normativity: the ability to be committed to standards of propriety, and to be motivated by them to act. The norms and standards to which we are committed[18] are those to which we hold ourselves and our world accountable. They also provide us with reasons to act when sufficiently violated. Our capacity for normative evaluation is the hallmark of our selfhood. But it is only when we translate our evaluations into reasoned action, that we achieve full human agency. As when we undertake to change our ways when found to violate our norms, or redefine a conceptual norm when violated by a state of affairs it was thought to represent. The two, as noted in the previous section, are interestingly inverted, when we experience shame it is the violating behavior that is condemned and changed, but when we laugh, it is the violated conceptual norm that is found guilty and amended.

In that case, when our norms fail to apply to what they are meant to, how do we know what's to blame? How do we know whether to modify the norm at play, or to correct whatever violated it? How do we distinguish between a normative failure and a failed norm? The major problem that animated Chap. 5 is the seeming incoherence of the very idea of self-faulting normative commitments; that we cannot pass normative judgment on norms to which we are committed, because it is by appeal to them that we pass such judgment. When something we do violates one of our norms, it is what we have done that we shamefully condemn, not the norm it violated. In humor, by contrast, it is always the violated (conceptual) norm that is ridiculed and made to take the blame. And as if to confirm the answer proposed in Chap. 5 to the problem of normative self-critique, our ability to be humored, as we have just seen, requires an external interlocutor.

As a form of judgment, humility amounts to an honest owning up to one's limitations and weaknesses. But it is when that sobering judgment is endorsed as a reason, and employed in practical reasoning that our reliance on others comes into full view as a major constituent of our very rationality. When an initial critical judgment yields a reasoned plan of action, rationality calls for a reflective assessment of our ability to rise to the occasion, which, when it proves negative, yields in turn a

---

[18] As opposed to undertaking faithfully to obey such a standard for ulterior reasons, such as because people expect you to, or because the law requires it.

second-order reasoned plan of action to seek and outsource what's needed to be done to someone better-suited for the task. Humility, though a reflexive and self-directed emotion, induces us to look outward in appreciation of human diversity and of those endowed differently than we are.

When humility motivates agential action, it serves willy-nilly to position us among and aware of others, but it does so very differently from most other socializing forces. Acting mindfully of others is mostly motivated by shared membership in a group. The bonds that relate us to other members of our families, classes, communities and societies also mark us off from those who are not. Our special affinity to them is based on sameness or similarity; on what we feel we have in common with them, and when we contemplate acting, we take them into consideration as such.

When humility motivates us to take action, we act mindfully of those endowed with what we lack for the task at hand; attentive to what we do *not* have in common with them; deeming their very otherness a valuable asset. Even at its most rudimentary form, humility transforms self-critical reflection into a genuine valuing of those from whom we crucially differ, *because* we crucially differ from them! However, what are valued in such cases are differences in training, endowment, talent, skill, and know-how, not differences of opinion, culture, or commitment. Our world is complex and, at any given moment, doing what needs to be done requires a division of labor, much of it specific and skilled.[19] The notion of otherness at play here is more practical and functional than it is normative. And the notion of value at play in such cases is real yet impersonal. The availability of a professional to deal with a problem is valued for obvious reasons by those affected by it, but not necessarily by the unqualified person who draws attention to it while humbly declining to solve it herself (unless she happens to be effected by it too).

But the point at which we humbly own up to our inability, in principle, to hold our normative commitments themselves in self-normative check except when criticized by others, is the point at which the otherness we come to value acquires normative depth that has nothing to do with training, skill or talent. And, because the problem of normative self-critique is wholly internal and entirely ours, the value of otherness it entails is also rendered wholly personal. And because both the problem

---

[19] Rabbinic literature gives powerful expression to such valuing of human diversity in the special blessing one is supposed to recite when witnessing a large throng of people:

> Blessed be the One who created all of these people to serve me. How much did the first man have to toil before he could taste even one mouthful? He had to plant, plough, reap, bind sheaves, thresh, winnow, select, grind, sift, knead, and bake, and only after that could he eat. And I wake up each the morning and find all my food already prepared. How much did the first man have to toil before he wore a shirt? He have to shear, wash, comb, dye, spin, weave, and sew, and only then could he wear it. And I wake up each morning and find all of my clothes already made. How many skilled laborers are anxious to rise early to sell their goods, and I wake up each morning and find all their goods already made. (Babylonian Talmud, *Berakhot*, 58a)

of normative self-critique and human normative diversity are human universals, otherness should be not merely tolerated, but treasured, sought and cherished by all. Not for moral, but for rational reasons; motivated, not by a fundamental obligation we have to others, but by a fundamental mutual obligation we each have to ourselves!

7.3.1 Accomplishing the Tricolor

The idea that it is impossible to live to our full rational capacity without seriously engaging real others; that limiting the conversation about what we value and care for to similarly committed fellow-travelers can never get us beyond our normative commitments; that the potential transformative impact of dialogue is directly proportional to the level of *disagreement* it breaches, is of highly significant *political* importance that is yet to be properly appreciated. Avishai Margalit speaks for many in claiming that although

> ... the revolutionary triangle *liberté, égalité, fraternité* ... in a way set the agenda for all modern political thought. Almost all the effort in political thought has been devoted to two sides of the triangle, liberty and equality, and especially to the relationship between them. Indeed, one can view justice as finding the right balance between liberty and equality. The neglected side of the revolutionary triangle is fraternity.

"Some modern liberals," he goes on to argue, "view fraternity as pernicious communitarianism, a threat to our core sense of individuality," which he views as a grave mistake. Fraternity, he submits, "is important as a motivating force to bring about liberty and equality. Only a society with a strong sense of fraternity has the potential to bring about justice" (Margalit 2017, 1–2). Focusing on betrayal (on dealing with fraternity "through its pathology"), he merely states these claims about the importance of fraternity *for* liberty and equality, full aware "that there is nothing obvious" about them, but goes no further. Others have, perhaps most prominently Nussbaum who devoted an entire book, Nussbaum (2013), subtitled: "Why Love matters to Justice" to developing an account of national fraternity within the framework of Rawlsian political liberalism.[20]

Taking her cue from Tagore and Mill, Nussbaum's solution involves cultivating patriotic feelings of belonging to a shared benign national home by means of national rituals and art. In the shared rituals of civic religion like Martin Luther King's day, she writes, "people of many different religions and other identities may be brought together around a common set of values through the power of art and symbol. ... Shared grief – whether on the Gettysburg battlefield or at the Vietnam Veterans Memorial ... Songs of national pride and aspiration have a similar capacity to forge or re-forge identity."[21]

---

[20] Rawls (2005).

[21] Nussbaum (2013, 388). Nussbaum casts her net much wider in her ambitious attempt to delineate the complexity of conceptual, cultural, artistic and especially educational means for cultivating the

Such rituals may create civil closeness, but are incapable of fostering respect, worth, or love of forms of life contrary to one's own, and certainly do not render otherness or real diversity in any way desirable. Commitment to them as to the ideals and arrangements that ensure civil freedom and equality are capable at most of slightly thickening the thin civic ground *shared* by the nation's diverse communities. But it can contribute little to fostering a thick social *fraternité* with those whose lifeworlds others deem to be not only alien, but profoundly wrong.

Popper (1966) aspires to go in a more promising direction, which he leaves, however, vexingly underdeveloped. *The Open Society*'s positive master idea is that diversified societies are preferable to the more monolithic variety, because of the mutually enriching challenge that communities differently committed pose one another. But writing under the heavy cloud of WWII, the Jewish Viennese refugee, exiled to a country he loathed, devoted his massive tome far more to criticizing the open society's totalitarian enemies than to developing the idea of the open society itself, which he barely sketches.

Popper rightly locates the true value of real difference, not in what diverse cultures find they share as co-citizens, nor in the values of the political framework that grants them the liberty to lead their chosen lives, as Nussbaum has it, but in the stimulating environment they create by the critically challenging one another. Popper, however, leaves it at that, oblivious as to why anyone would seek for such challenges, as well as to the question of how transformative dialogue is at all possible across great normative divides.[22] Indeed Popper not only begged all the questions he raised in that book, but thereafter spent a lifetime convincing himself that at least in science normative diversity was a myth![23]

But if there is any truth in the argument presented here, namely, that, as much as we would like to, we are unable, in principle, to step outside ourselves and take normative critical stock of our identity-forming commitments, except when seriously challenged by significant others, then all the questions Popper failed to address in his book, as well as what he saw fit to deny in later work, can be fully addressed. First, the idea of an open society it yields is akin to Rawls's political liberalism—a state committed to the equality and liberty of its culturally diverse national collective to whose different concepts of the good it remains aloof and equally supportive.

---

kind of love between fellow citizens that she believes "matters for justice". She identifies such love primarily with compassion, and engages a breathtaking array of literary, musical, psychological and philosophical works, in theorizing the infantile beginnings, the bodily and erotic manifestations, the playfulness, gender-based elements, and much more capable of extending feelings of compassion from family, ethnos and creed, to the entire body-politic. This is not the place for a detailed evaluation of whether her extraordinary undertaking succeeds or fails in merging its many strands into a coherent picture of civic love. As I argue in the following pages, I believe that a major emotional element goes missing in the mix she presents.

[22] A question answered shortly after with a firm "no!" by a broad array of prominent voices including Wittgenstein (1972, 81e), Carnap (2002, prt.4, B), Kuhn (1962), and Rorty (1989).

[23] *The Myth of the Framework: In Defense of Science and Rationality*, is the unfounded title (alluding most probably to Sellars's "Myth of the Given") Popper (1994), the last collection of essays he published, almost 50 years after *The Open Society*.

7.4 Buridan's Meta-Ass

But with an important difference. Its commitment to equality and liberty is grounded, not in the metaphysics of universal human rights (which, of course, it need not deny!), but in humble recognition of the unique *value* of cultural diversity and the state's duty and interest in ensuring and maintaining it. It is a view of society and the obligations of government based on the master idea that humans are indeed created equal, not in the usual sense of the term (which, of course, need not be denied!), but *equally incapable* of living up to their full human, culturally diverse capacities, except in dialogical interaction with significant others.

Second, and most importantly, unlike any other form of humble outsourcing, such a view of our dependency on others is at once universal, symmetrical and bilateral. That is because otherness is of itself symmetrical and bilateral. Any person's need for the critical input of others committed differently by definition delineates their need for hers—a symmetry nicely captured by Sellars's and Brandom's image of playing the game of giving and asking for reasons.[24] As long, of course, that it is played (a) across dividing lines of substantial normative differences, and (b) that it is played for mutual critique, rather than for the sake of mere scorekeeping or even mutual recognition. This what lends it its forceful political potential.

7.4 Buridan's Meta-Ass[25]

To become ambivalent toward a norm or a standard, the terminal value of a final end, or a once beloved or despised person, place, regime or work of art, is to deem them normatively undecided. Becoming of two minds about something once valued is not to deem it flawed. What is rendered problematic and in need of mending by such a change of attitude—according to Frankfurt, urgently so—is the self itself!

Because what we love, according to Frankfurt, is what we want our wills to want, a person's care for his beloved, is "tantamount ... to caring about himself. ... Someone who loves justice, for instance, necessarily wants to be a person who serves the interests of justice... [who] necessarily regards serving its interests not only as contributing to the realization of a desirable social condition, but also as integral to the realization of his ideal for himself" (Frankfurt 1999, 139.)

Normative ambivalence, he writes, represents "a rupture in [one's] inner cohesion or unity; it means there is a division within [one's] will" (139) consisting "in a vacillation or opposition within the self which guarantees that one volitional

---

[24] Because inherently mutual, our shared need for the critique of real others as the only means we have for attaining our full rational capacity, cannot be deemed morally reprehensible on a Kantian showing. Realizing our need for, and actively seeking other people's critical input, is willy-nilly to recognize their need for ours and to willingly offer it. This is not a form of instrumental employment, but, as in the case of all bilateral needs, a recipe for true fraternity. I am grateful to Reiner Forst for raising this point while presenting an earlier version of the argument in the course of my Dagmar Westberg Lectures at the Goethe University, Frankfurt, in January 2020.

[25] The following several paragraphs take their cue from Fisch and Benbaji (2011, 264–271).

element will be opposed to the other, so that the person cannot avoid acting against himself" (ibid.) A person unable to free himself of the conflict, and persists in a state of ambivalence is, therefore, "volitionally fragmented. His will is unstable and incoherent, moving him in contrary directions simultaneously or in a disorderly sequence. ... his will, therefore, lacks effective guiding authority." Such a person "is at odds with himself" (Frankfurt 2004, 92). Frankfurt views ambivalence as a grave disorder that demands urgent attention; "a disease of the mind"that "tends to alarm a person and to mobilize him for an attempt at 'self-preservation'" (2006, 95). When in a state of ambivalence a person runs up against "a quite primitive human need to establish and maintain volitional unity". Ambivalence is a threat to that unity, a "threat to the cohesion of the self." (ibid).

The problem with ambivalence, one might say, is that it represents a significant *weakening* of a person's capacity to conduct himself rationally. Being of two minds about a norm, a standard, or a final end renders all relevant judgment impossibly incoherent. If the necessities of wholehearted normative commitment provide the basis for a person's volitional rationality and hence the grounds for practical reasoning, then, by the same token, ambivalence generates *volitional irrationality* which in turn obliterates his very capacity for agency in the affected areas. The deep and urgent need to free ourselves of ambivalence is no less than an insistent self-rallying to reclaim our rationality.

But, as I have argued earlier, in one important sense, wholly overlooked by Frankfurt, Taylor and Jaeggi, normative ambivalence can be a rare blessing. At one level an ambivalated norm is a demoted norm, an obligating norm no more, and, therefore, an impediment to our capacity to reason rationally from and by means of it. But at the same time, by virtue of its temporary loss of normative standing, it is rendered normatively criticizable by the person whose norm it just was. Detrimental as Frankfurt would have us believe normative ambivalence can be, especially with regard to major commitments, there is a deep sense in which it is rational, in fact supremely rational, to actively seek to be rendered temporarily ambivalent toward major norms, because that is only way for us to take normative critical stock of them. Only in a state of normative ambivalence can our commitments be rationally invigorated or reformed.

I ended the previous chapter realizing that contrary to what I had thought for many years, there may be a another way of proactively opening oneself to normative ambivalation other than deliberate exposure to external critique. Despite having taken firm stands both against Rorty's despair of their being any such way to do so, as well as against Jaeggi's criticism of Frankfurt's two-tiered self, I have now come to realize that while Jaeggi was wrong about second-order volitions, she was right about second-order emotions, and that there was a way of reading Rorty as unwittingly enabling arguing against, not merely ironically doubting, one's final vocabulary.

Rorty, to recall, describes the strong poet as experimenting with other forms of life, experiencing how others live, reading many books, acquainting herself with other final vocabularies. This is different from joining the reasons game to invite criticism. For it is not about exploring what people committed differently think of

7.4 Buridan's Meta-Ass

her. Rorty never imagined that external normative critique could have the desired effect. Nonetheless, it is probably the best way (other than taking deliberate unreasonable risks) to be caught off guard by newly experienced situations liable to provoke a substantial emotional response. And when such a response is rewarded by an immediate disapproving, "come again" second-order emotion, we find ourselves normatively ambivalated.

And again, just as in the case of external critique, even when knowingly motivated to do so by humbly acknowledging the limits of normative self-criticism, and hence, engaging in a supreme act of personal rationality, it is a task no one can perform alone or in the company of like-minded others. Which brings us to the third and final chapter of the Bible's insightful account of the creation of humankind as fully-fledged partners capable of creating and taking responsibility for their world.

7.4.1 A Final Biblical Interlude

The previous chapters of the Hebrew Bible's account of the creation of humankind saw the birth of human selfhood in Adam and Eve realizing and attempting to cover their nakedness, and that of human normativity in Cain's realizing and regretting his sin. Both stories are commonly read simplistically (and uninterestingly) as mere episodes of sin and divine retribution. Adam and Eve indeed disobeyed God in eating from the forbidden tree and were punished accordingly, but shame of being exposed naked, as I have argued, is a primary feeling of self-failure that has nothing to do with sin or punishment. The "knowledge of good and evil" it imparted on them was the uniquely human ability to view and maintain their bodies and minds as private and personal domains of self-regulated control.

Cain's killing of Abel, we saw, marked the birth of human normativity capable of both transcending and curbing animal kingdom's struggle for survival and procreation (and in the human world, the struggle for divine attention). The coupling of agency and normative commitment allowed humankind to use God's creation as the template for creating their own world of habitat, technologies, culture, and even religion (Gen. 4:17, 20–22, 26).

I locate the third and last divinely directed and emotionally significant chapter in the Bible's account of the birth of humanity in the well-known story of the Tower of Babel (Gen. 11). Against the bleak backdrop of Noah's total lack of initiative, the city and tower constitute, one might say, the first biblical case of a large-scale human project explicitly undertaken for a reason:

> And the whole earth was of one language, and of one speech. And it came to pass... that they found a plain in the land of Shinar; and they dwelt there...And they said... let us build us a city and a tower, whose top may reach unto heaven; and let us make us a name, lest we be scattered abroad upon the face of the whole earth. (11:1–4)

God, we are told, sees their initiative for what it is:

> Behold, the people is one, and they have all one language; and this they have schemed to do, and now nothing will be withheld from them, which they have schemed to do (6)

Because all humankind speaks one language and holds similar opinions, once they form a scheme and apply themselves to it, there is nothing to stop them. Caught in the fixated confines of what Janis (1972) (following Orwell) nicely dubs "groupthink", the agents of "the whole earth" earnestly applied their capacity for normative appraisal to critically assess their situation, detect its weak points and set about in earnest to better their lot. What better for a unanimous, like-minded society marching to the beat of the same drum than to define themselves as such (make themselves a collective name) by congregating in the mutually justifying huddle of a single city marked by a tower to signal and announce their presence? To which God reacted by realizing their deepest fears.

> Come, lets us go down and confound their language, that they may not understand one another's speech. So the Lord scattered them abroad from there upon the face of the earth: and they ceased to build the city. (7–8)

Most read the famous story as yet another tale of human sin and rebellion and cruel divine punishment, despite the fact that the biblical account of their plan and reasoning contains no hint of it being endorsed rebelliously or in defiance of God's will. But if there is any truth in my analysis of the normative limits of rational groupthink, then

(a) The very existence of normative diversity is rendered an invaluable blessing, for it is only in the company of significant others that we can live to our full rational capacity. From which follows,

(b) That the epitome of rationality is to be humbly aware of our inability, in principle, to hold our normative commitments in critical check, and to proactively outsource the task to others by seeking and inviting their critique.

Viewed thus, the story of the Tower of Babel takes on a whole new meaning. Rather than another episode-cycle of human sin and divine penalty, it can now be seen as the last chapter in the creation of our fully-fledged humanity. Concentrated on the plains of Shinar and marching to the single unreflective drum of a shared "final vocabulary", the fledgling human race enlists in a reasoned, large-scale, ambitious, if senseless, collective undertaking of its own desire and design. God intervenes, albeit ruthlessly, not to punish them, but to offer them something that in their localized and overly cohesive state they were incapable in principle of even realizing its significance: a potentially ambivalating, and hence potentially transformative, diversity of locale, culture, norm, attitude and opinion. On such a showing, by scattering the newly settled city dwellers and introducing a diversity of human language, and human norm, God can be said to have saved humanity from a life of dogmatic, single-minded normative fixation. One can still decide to close oneself off to the challenging voices of other forms of life and experience, but that is, from now on, a matter of choice rather than fate.

7.5 The We in the I

Let me stress that there is nothing apologetic in my readings of the three biblical episodes as positive, constructive episodes of human creation. In them God is indeed envisaged as knowingly manipulating Adam and Eve, then Cain, and finally, the survivors of the flood, to develop and realize their full human potential. But in all three cases it is an extremely excruciating, manipulative, and cruelly forced process. As especially Christian readings of the Garden of Eden story bear grim witness, Adam and Eve's acquisition of human selfhood came at the heavy price of believing that they had drastically fallen from grace and forever punished. For the emergence of Cain's normativity, God was willing to knowingly sacrifice Abel! And one can only imagine the horrifying shattering of the post-traumatic survivor's communal fabric, social structure, and lifework necessary to create cultural diversity. Perhaps God had no choice but to act so ruthlessly, but act ruthlessly he did. Here, however, my interest in the three biblical texts has focused on their anthropological, rather than theological significance; on the three-stage story of the creation of humanity, rather than on the nature of God's role in it.

7.5 The We in the I[26]

The essentially Frankfurtian picture of human selfhood alluded to and developed in the this essay envisages two related yet very different ideas of a we in the I—one inherently *intra*subjective and one equally inherently *inter*subjective or relational.[27] The plurality that grounds the individual self pertains to the fundamental split between our desired and empirical selves, an exclusively human split that enables self-consciousness, reflectivity and normativity, and that jointly endows our desired self, our I-part, with the authority to speak for us in the first person, to impose its (second-order) will on who we are, to supply us with reasons to think and act, and to call us to task when we fail to live up to its standards.[28]

Our I-part, the seat of our normative commitments, is what furnishes our capacity to act rationally, namely to hold ourselves and our world accountable to the norms and standards we are committed to, and act within our power to put right what we deem to be sufficiently wrong to merit intervening. But rationality demands, I have argued, that rational action be undertaken rationally; that the demand to hold ourselves and our world accountable to our norms and standards and commit

---

[26] This section knowingly borrows its title from Axel Honneth (2012). Had I made it the title of the entire book (which would have been wholly inappropriate), I may well have also retained its subtitle, while using 'Recognition,' not in the Hegelian sense developed by Honneth, but as denoting the need for mutual recognition of the indispensable value of real otherness.

[27] Frankfurt himself, of course, only acknowledged the first of the two.

[28] Again, on the conspicuous omission of this post-Kantian picture of human selfhood in Williams's otherwise splendid *Shame and Necessity*—both as a modern contrast to the Greek conceptions of personhood he purports to expose, or, conversely, as the picture of modern selfhood he claims they embody—see Sect. 3.3.3 above.

98   7 All Together Now

ourselves to endorsing our critical findings as reasons for reformative action, extends to our norms and standards themselves and to how we apply them.

Brandom, we have seen,[29] believed that our critical obligations toward the body of our commitments are fully met by trouble-shooting them for coherence and consistency.[30] But that, I have argued, cannot be enough. Given the diversity of human normative commitment, the demand of rationality is that we deem our commitments to be worthy of our commitment, not merely to form a coherent and consistent whole. To that end, like anything else in the purview of our responsibility, they must be found to pass normative critical muster. And that, we have seen cannot be accomplished alone.

What renders humankind ultimately unique is our ability to apply our agency to standing back from ourselves in self judgment—from the boundaries we set to our very selves, from the conceptual vocabularies and normative commitments by which we conceive, perceive, and estimate, from our strengths and weaknesses, and from the verdict of our emotional responses. Like all emotions, the four orders of reflexive emotion we have looked at here represent spontaneous evaluative reactions to such sobering self-realizations. These, we have seen, jointly define what sets us apart as human: our agency, our sapience, our normativity, and rationality, our ability to critically self-reflect. But at the same time, each of them demonstrates dramatically how in all these respects *realizing our very personhood necessarily positions us with respect to others*, without whom we are incapable of attaining our full potential.

- Primary shame is experienced when the intricate boundaries of our personal privacy are violated, and with them the complex and self-defining economy of concealment and revelation by which we position ourselves with respect to others. By means of this primordial act of agency, we determine, not if, but how exactly the we defines the I.
- Secondary shame in its most pristine form pertains to the often strained, intrasubjective dialogue between the two parts of the human self—the we within the I—the we that literally constitutes the two-tiered human I, and is felt when we admonish ourselves for failing to live up to norms we hold to. But at times, as in the Sartre-Halbertal peeping Tom example, to experience secondary shame the we must be externalized, and one needs to be caught off-guard in the disturbingly disapproving gaze of an external witness.
- The ability to enjoy a joke, I have argued following Schopenhauer's lead, goes to the heart of our uniquely human conceptual abilities (our very sapience, as Brandom defines it), or rather to the precise point at which the generalizing power of our concepts inevitably fails us. The beauty of humor's pointed lessons is their harmlessness. Despite forcefully exemplifying how gravely misleading our only means of cognitive extrapolation can be, joking does so not by making

---

[29] See Sect. 5.3, n. 15 above and accompanying text.

[30] For a similar view see Bratman (2006), and Tollefsen (2007) who builds on and away from Bratman.

us suffer the consequences, but by allowing us to experience the discrepancy with an amusing jolt. And as if to prove that because our languages are socially shared collectivities, and their limitations, therefore, universal, joking too necessarily and wholly transcends the boundaries of the individual self. It takes someone else to tell us a joke.

- Humility's universal highpoint, we have seen, marks rationality's universal highpoint. Rationality demands that we intervene to change our minds, ways and world whenever they violate our norms and standards. Rationality also demands that we intervene to replace our norms and standards whenever *they* fail to pass normative critical muster. But how can we rationally change our minds about the norms and standards by which we change our minds? We cannot. Left to our own devices it is impossible for us to normatively criticize the norms that serve us to normatively criticize. Humility's highpoint is to humbly own up to this universally shared human inadequacy. Rationality's highpoint comes with the humble realization that exposure to external criticism can ambivalate us sufficiently to self-critique the norms it challenges, and to, therefore, actively seek such exposure.
- Rationality at its best is thus seen to yield far more than the Kantian imperative to view others as having the right to be deemed ends in themselves, and oneself as belonging to the Kingdom of Ends. Rationality at its best bestows universally unique and categorical *value* on their very otherness. From a rational point of view, normative diversity is not something to be rationally overcome, as Kant and many latter-day Kantians argue, but to be seen as a rare and necessary blessing.
- Finally, our ability to develop second-order emotions—itself, a wonderful example of human emotive reflexivity—especially of the disapproving variety, teaches us that new and unexpected experiences can also have an ambivalating, and, therefore, a normatively self-critical impact on our commitments. But because such emotionally perplexing experiences always take us by surprise, they can hardly be deliberately pursued. Still, when knowingly exposing ourselves to people and communities who think and judge differently, we will find ourselves challenged and liable to be ambivalated not only by their actual criticism, but by their forms of life more generally.

Bibliography

Brandom RB (1994) Making it explicit: reasoning, representing and discursive commitment. Harvard University Press, Cambridge, MA

Brandom RB (2000) Articulating reasons: an introduction to inferentialism. Harvard University Press, Cambridge, MA

Bratman ME (2006) Dynamics of sociality. Midwest Studies in Philosophy 30:1–15

Buzaglo M (2001) The logic of concept expansion. Cambridge University Press, Cambridge

Carnap R (2002) The logical syntax of language. Open Court, Chicago

Fisch M, Benbaji Y (2011) The view from within: normativity and the limits of self-criticism. University of Notre Dame Press, South Bend

Frankfurt HG (1999) Necessity, Volition, and Love. CambridgeUniversity Press, Cambridge

Frankfurt HG (2004) The reasons of love. Princeton University Press, Princeton

Frankfurt HG (2006) Taking ourselves seriously and getting it right. Stanford University Press, Stanford

Honneth A (2012) The I in the we: studies in the theory of recognition. Polity Press, Cambridge

Janis IL (1972) Victims of groupthink: a psychological study of foreign-policy decisions and fiascoes. Houghton Mifflin Harcourt, Boston

Kuhn TS (1962) The structure of scientific revolutions. University of Chicago Press, Chicago

Lakatos I (1976) Proofs and refutations: the logic of mathematical discovery. Cambridge University Press, Cambridge

Margalit A (2017) On Betrayal. Harvard University Press, Cambridge, MA

Nussbaum MC (2004) Hiding from humanity: shame, disgust, and the law. Princeton University Press, Princeton

Nussbaum MC (2010) From disgust to humanity: sexual orientation and constitutional law. Oxford University Press, Oxford

Nussbaum MC (2012) The new religious intolerance: overcoming the politics of fear in an anxious age. Harvard University Press, Cambridge, MA

Nussbaum MC (2013) Political emotions: why love matters to justice. Harvard University Press, Cambridge, MA

Nussbaum MC (2016) Anger and forgiveness: resentment, generosity, justice. Oxford University Press, Oxford

Nussbaum MC (2018) The monarchy of fear: a philosopher looks at our political crisis. Simon and Schuster, New York

Popper KR (1966) The open society and its enemies, 2 vols. 5th edn. Routledge & Kegan Paul, London

Popper KR (1994) The myth of the framework: in defense of science and rationality. Routledge, Abingdon

Rawls J (2005) Political liberalism, revised and expanded edn. Columbia University Press, New York

Rorty R (1989) Contingency, irony, solidarity. Cambridge University Press, Cambridge

Sellars W (1962) Philosophy and the scientific image of man. In: Colodny RG (ed) Frontiers of science and philosophy. University of Pittsburgh Press, Pittsburgh, pp 35–78

Taylor C (1985a) Human agency and language: philosophical papers, vol I. Cambridge University Press, Cambridge

Taylor G (1985b) Pride, shame and guilt. Oxford University Press, Oxford

Taylor C (2016) The language animal: the full shape of human linguistic capacity. Harvard University Press, Cambridge, MA

Tollefsen DP (2007) Group deliberation, social cohesion, and scientific teamwork: is there room for dissent? Episteme 3:37–51

Wittgenstein L (1922) Tractatus Logicus Philosophicus (with Introduction by B Russell). Keagan Paul, Trench, Trubner & Co., London

Wittgenstein L (1972) On certainty (English-German edition, Anscombe GEM and von Wright GH (eds)). Harper and Row, New York

Index

A
Ability to enjoy the comic, 98
Acting for a reason, 53
    to claim the authority to intervene, 53
    to take responsibility for evaluating a
        situation, 53
Adam and Eve, 80, 95
    birth of human selfhood, 95
    birth of primary shame, 80
    eating from the tree of knowledge, 80
        paradox of religious anthropology, 81
    Hiding from God, 81
Agency, 2, 19
Ambivalence, 94
    "disease of the mind", 94
    a threat to the cohesion of the self, 94
Amusement, 29
Aristotle, 31
Augustin, 14
Authenticity, 67

B
Barrett, L.F., 4
Berger, P., 32
Bergson, H., 30, 35–36, 39
    incongruity theory of humor, 36
Bloom, H., 74
    anxiety of influence, 75
    fear of unoriginality, 74
Brain research, 3
    neurophysiological reduction, 5

Brandom, R.B., 40, 47, 48, 53–55, 65, 85,
    86, 93, 98
    definition of sapience, 98
Buzaglo, M., 88

C
Cain, 80, 95
    and the birth of human normativity, 83
    constitutive moment of normative
        self-admonishment, 82
    killing of Abel, 81, 95
        believed it the right thing to do, 82
        the birth of murder, 81
Capacity for normative evaluation, 89
    the hallmark of human selfhood, 89
Carnap, R., 40
City Dionysia, 33
Cognitivist *vs.* noncognitivist accounts of
    emotion, 3
Cognitivist view of emotion, 7
Come again effect of a second-order emotion, 73
Comical, 29–41
Commitment, 25
Common law judge, 54
Concepts, 50
Conceptual engineering, 87
Conceptualization, 37
Conceptual language, 37, 85, 86
Criticism, 2, 18, 51
    contains a measure of rebuke, 18
    to criticize resembles an existence proof, 51

© The Editor(s) (if applicable) and The Author(s), under exclusive license to
Springer Nature Switzerland AG 2025
M. Fisch, *Reflexive Emotions*, SpringerBriefs in Philosophy,
https://doi.org/10.1007/978-3-031-83764-7

D
DeLancey, C., 3
Dennett, D., 4
Dependency on others, 93
  at once universal, symmetrical and
    bilateral, 93
Descartes, R., 40
Desires are not emotions, 20
Dialogue, 75
  transformative potential, 75
Disobedience, 80
  miscalculation not a normative failure, 80
Divine laughter, 33

E
Eco, U., 31
  the Name of Rose, 31
Emotional ambivalence, 52
Emotional responses, 63
  expressive of inherently normative
    judgments, 63
Emotions, 8, 32, 62, 65, 77
  are not arguments, 64
  between mindful purpose and mindless
    compulsion, 65
  can be reasoned with, 32
  cannot be undertaken for a reason, 62
  emotion *vs.* volition, 62–64
  as a form of personal judgment, 48
  function as reasons for acting, 64
  harbors motive force but not logical force, 65
  never deliberated or considered, 62
  as normative rather than eudaimonistic
    Judgments, 8
  norm-laden, 64
  as perspectival judgment, 8
  spontaneous and involuntary, 62
  unreasoned evaluative judgments, 64
  unreasoned motivating force, 77
Eudaimonism, 7, 63
Evolution, 5, 9
External criticism, 95
External normative criticism, 73
  ambivalating effect of, 73
  transformative potential, 57
    analogous to playback device, 58

F
First- and second-order emotions, 10
First-order desires, 20, 63
  are not judgments, 63

Force of reasons, 3
Forst, R., 93
Framework dependencey, 50
Frankfurt, H., 18, 20, 22, 61, 84, 93, 94, 97
  account of the split human self, 20
  volitional necessity, 72
Freud, S., 34
  tripartite theory of laughter, 34
Friedman, M., 40
Fuchs, T., 4

G
Game of giving and asking for reasons, 47, 93
  epitome of rationality, 47, 53, 55
  supervenes on self-doubt, criticism and
    justification, 55
Game-theoretical accounts of rationality, 8
Griffiths, P., 3
Groupthink, 96

H
Halbertal, M., 11, 13–25, 78
  primary *vs.* secondary shame, 11
  primitive shame, 11
Harré, R., 3
Hegel, G.W.F., 48
  mutual recognition, 48
Hobbes, T., 34
Honneth, A., 97
Human and animal emotion, 7, 63
Human emotions, 8
Human reflexivity, 49
Human selfhood, 3
Human selfhood and agency, 79
  the ability to stand back, take stock, and
    respond to ourselves, 79
Humiliation, 11
Humility, 1, 11, 19, 43–45, 89, 90, 99
  and appreciation of human diversity, 90
  constructively self-critical, 43
  different from modesty, 44
  as emotion, 43–46, 48
  as guide to inaction, 45
  vs. humiliation, 44
  motivates acting mindfully of those
    endowed differently, 90
  owning up to limitations, 48
  owning up to shortcomings, 44
  pathologies of, 45
  as reflexive emotion, 47
  role in rationality, 47

Index

role of normativity, 49
seldomly entails self-rebuke, 48–49
uptake of candid self-assessment, 44
Humor, 1, 31, 85, 89
deemed inferior, 31
as failing of self-expression, 85
Humorous, 29
Hypergoods, 69

I

Incongruity theories of humor, 35–39
Intentional laughter, 36, 88
as reflexive emotion, 88
requires dialogical setting, 88
Intimacy, 9, 15
I-part, 21, 49, 51, 54, 64, 84, 85
personal identify, 84
as seat of norms and standards, 49
as seat of second order volitions, 49
speaking in the first-person, 84

J

Jaeggi, R., 18, 53, 61, 67, 94
problem of alienation, 67
Jaeggi's criticism of Frankfurt, 94
Jaeggi vs. Frankfurt, 66–68
Jealousy, 83
not a reflexive emotion, 83
Joke is irredeemably ruined by
explaining it, 31
Judging vs. arguing, 64–66

K

Kant, I., 15, 35, 37, 54, 99
categorical imperative, 15, 99
incongruity theory of humor, 35
Kingdom of Ends, 99
Kenny, A., 3
Korsgaard, C., 24
Kuhn, T., 40

L

Lakatos, I., 88
monster-adjustment and monster-
barring, 88
Laughter, 30
as co-produced, 40
Leys, R., 3
Liberté, égalité, fraternité, 91

M

MacIntyre, A., 53
Margalit, A., 91
McDowell, J., 40, 65
Mill, J.S., 91
Mixed feelings, 62, 66

N

National fraternity, 92
Non-reflexive shame, 25–26
shame for others, 25
Normative ambivalence, 57, 58,
70, 73, 93
a necessary and sufficient
condition for normative
self-critique, 73
Normative commitment, 3
Normative diversity, 49, 96
Normative diversity and self-critique: human
universals, 91
Normative failure vs. a failed norm, 89
Normative prioritizing, 52, 70
Normative self-approval, 64
uninterestingly circular, 64
Normative self-critique, 64
Normative self-evaluation, 49
as a form of self-alienation, 49
Normativity, 2, 9, 89
Norms and standards of propriety, 8
Notions of otherness, 90
Nussbaum, M., 3, 6, 7, 9, 12, 13, 16, 19, 43,
63, 77, 78, 83, 91
civic love, 92
cognitivist view of emotion, 7
eudaimonistic judgments, 7
emotions in politics and the law, 7
evolutionary concerns, 9
Hiding from Humanity, 13
primitive shame, 18, 19
unconvincing, 13

O

Obedience, 80
a matter of utility not propriety, 80
Only humans can appreciate a joke, 30
The Open Society, 92
Orwell, G., 96
Otherness, 90
and normative depth, 90
should be treasured, sought and
cherished, 91

P

Paradox, 56
Plato, 31, 36, 37
  cave allegory, 37
Political liberalism, 92
Popper, K.R., 19, 40, 92
Practical reasoning, 94
Primary shame, 13–17, 78, 80, 81, 84, 98
  and human selfhood and agency, 78
Primitive shame, 12–14, 83
Privacy and self, 15
The problem of normative self-critique, 52
Prudent criticism, 51
  aims to be endorsed as self-criticism, 51
  leveled from its addressees'
    perspective, 51
  to an extent untruthfull, 57
Punchline, 88
  must be delivered by somebody else, 88

R

Rational action, 46
  as action taken for a reason, 46
  humility a necessary constituent of rational
    action, 47
Rationality, 2, 47, 51, 99
  universal highpoint, 99
Rationality and critique, 46–48
  outsourcing normative self-critique, 55
Rationality and humility, 50
  are human universals, 50
Rationality of action, 46
Rationality of belief, 46
Rawls, J., 91, 92
Raz, J., 53, 55
Reciprocal recognition, 53
Reflexive emotions, 2, 9, 78, 83
  exclusively human, 9
  indicative of our shared humanity, 78
  as normative self-evaluation, 10
  self-evaluation, 3
Reichenbach, H., 40
Relation between humiliation and
    humility, 11
Relation between shame and shaming, 11
Relief theories of the comic, 34
Responsibility, 18
Roman, M., 5
Rorty, R., 40, 74, 94
  final vocabulary, 74
  irony replaces rationality, 75
  strong poet, 74, 94

S

Sapience, 37
Sartre, J.-P., 14, 15
Schlick, M., 40
Schopenhauer, A., 29, 36–39, 85, 86, 98
  conception *vs.* perception, 38
  humor as conceptual failure, 39
  incongruity theory of humor, 36
    fares better than others, 40
  theory of concepts, 36
Schopenhauer's philosophy, 40
Scientific image, 4
Secondary shame, 14, 17, 21, 22, 80, 82, 84, 98
  Halbertal *vs.* Williams, 23
  when accused of normative self-failings, 21
Second-nature, 35
Second-order emotion, 1, 61–75, 99
  give rise to normative ambivalence, 71
  as moment of self-discovery and self-
    learning, 62
  as normative judgments of normative
    judgments, 63
  as opposed to second-order volitions, 63
  register surprise, 62
Second-order volitions, 20, 66, 67
  normative force of, 66
Self-alienation, 18, 68
Self-betrayal, 21
Self-consciousness, 18
Self-corrective self-rebuke, 20
Self-criticism, 19, 51
Self-critique, 3, 9
Self-defining standards, 21
Self-disapproval, 83
Selfhood, 16
  constituted by being seen and controling
    who sees what, 16
Self-identification, 68
Self-reproach, 19
Sellars, W., 4, 40, 47, 55, 65, 86, 92, 93
  manifest *vs.* scientific image, 86
Sentience, 37
Shame, 1, 11–26, 85, 88, 89
  and self-admonition, 19
Shame of nakedness, 3, 13, 23
Social norms, 78
Soloveitchik, J.B., 30, 31
Space of causes, 4
Space of reasons, 4, 53, 65
  as a space of (material) entailment, 65
Spencer, H., 34
Stendhal, K., 83
  holy envy, 83

Index

Subjectivity, 77
Superiority theories, 32
Synthetic unity of apperception, 54

T

Tagore, R., 91
Taylor, C., 4, 20, 53, 65, 69, 85, 94
    strong and weak evaluations, 20
Taylor, G., 23
Testing *vs.* criticizing, 18
Thick *vs.* thin evaluative concepts, 50
Tower of Babel Genesis 11, 95
    first biblical large-scale human project, 95
    third chapter in the creation of
        humanity, 96
Trusted criticism, 58
Tuomela, R., 26
    we-mode, 26

U

Universal human rights, 93

V

Value of cultural diversity, 93
Value of external criticism, 56
Value of otherness, 53–59, 90
Volitional irrationality, 94

W

Walzer, M., 26
    connected criticism, 26
Whitehead, A.N., 4
Williams, B., 2, 11, 14, 17, 18,
    23, 24, 97
    greek *vs.* modern concepts of
        selfhood, 24
    shame and necessity, 2, 11, 23
Wittgenstein, L., 53, 86
    private language argument, 53

Z

Zemach, E., 31
Zeno's paradoxes, 56